Shamanic Journeys Through the Caucasus

First published by O Books, 2009
O Books is an imprint of John Hunt Publishing Ltd., The Bothy, Deershot Lodge, Park Lane, Ropley, Hants, SO24 0BE, UK
office1@o-books.net
www.o-books.net

Distribution in:

UK and Europe
Orca Book Services
orders@orcabookservices.co.uk
Tel: 01202 665432 Fax: 01202 666219
Int. code (44)

USA and Canada
NBN
custserv@nbnbooks.com
Tel: 1 800 462 6420 Fax: 1 800 338 4550

Australia and New Zealand
Brumby Books
sales@brumbybooks.com.au
Tel: 61 3 9761 5535 Fax: 61 3 9761 7095

Far East (offices in Singapore, Thailand, Hong Kong, Taiwan)
Pansing Distribution Pte Ltd
kemal@pansing.com
Tel: 65 6319 9939 Fax: 65 6462 5761

South Africa
Alternative Books
altbook@peterhyde.co.za
Tel: 021 555 4027 Fax: 021 447 1430

Design: Stuart Davies

ISBN: 978 1 84694 253 2

A CIP catalogue record for this book is available from the British Library.

Printed by Digital Book Print

Shamanic Journeys Through the Caucasus

Michael Berman

BOOKS

Winchester, UK
Washington, USA

CONTENTS

Acknowledgements

I would like to thank Ana Ransom, a volunteer ESOL teacher for the charitable organization *Casa Latina*, for so kindly proof-reading and commenting on the first draft of the book.

If any copyright holders have been inadvertently overlooked, and for those copyright holders that all possible efforts have been made to contact but without success, the author will be pleased to make the necessary arrangements at the first opportunity.

The cover picture is a photo of an oil painting by Maka Bataishvili, an artist from the Republic of Georgia. For further details, please visit her website: www.makabatiashvili.net. Alternatively, if you are interested in buying any of her work and you are based in the UK, please visit www.caucasusarts.org.uk.

Introduction

Writers of all ranks, from belletrists to the titans of the Russian literary canon, have found inspiration in the Caucasus as a subject and a setting, including Lermentov, Pushkin, and Tolstoy. John Steinbeck can be included among their number too. During a visit in the late 1940s, he described it as "a magical place" and one that "becomes dream-like the moment you have left it" (see King, 2008, p.206). And anyone who has visited the region will have no hesitation in confirming this as it undoubtedly does leave you with the impression that you have been to another reality and back. *Shamanic Journeys through the Caucasus* explores the region from a different angle, through its folktales;

> The Caucasus is a land with which the earliest folklore of Europe is connected. One has only to think of the Argonauts and of Prometheus to be reminded of the long ages through which the mountainous country… between Europe and Asia, has been connected with man's inherent love of story-telling. Just as a map of the races of the Caucasus is variegated, showing more than sixty different people, so also is its folklore.
>
> …Whatsoever passed eastwards or westwards over the old trade or military routes, wither to north or south of the mountains, across the one ancient pass which leads over them, or along the western shore of the Caspian Sea - all these various migrations left people and things and spiritual influences among the rocks of the Caucasus that explains the variety of the Caucasian tales, the wealth of Caucasian folklore (Dirr, 1925, pp. v & vi).

It is also of course what makes the study of the tales so fascinating, the detective work that is required to trace the different influences that have helped to shape them and to turn them into what they now are.

Although generalizations, by their very nature, can only be of limited value, at the same time it would not be entirely misleading to assert that the Caucasus is, to all intents and purposes, "a single cultural landscape" in so much as "no part makes sense when separated from the others" (Ascherson, 2007, p.xiv) and this will be seen to be the case throughout this study.

On the other hand, it has also been claimed that

> The Caucasus has never been one place but many, including arid plains, semi-tropical foothills, craggy gorges, and alpine peaks. Moving through these varied landscapes – crossing rivers or coming down out of hills – literally meant exiting one world and entering another. The variety of topography and climate helps account for the multiplicity of political, cultural, and economic influences that have long defined the region (King, 2008, p.8)

The two quotations need not be mutually exclusive of course. What both the claims illustrate is that attempting to present a comprehensive picture of the region is by no means straight-forward, and that whoever does so is in effect "sticking their neck out". However sensitive one attempts to be when setting out on such a task, it is more or less inevitable someone will end up feeling aggrieved at, or misrepresented by, the result. Therefore, let me apologize in advance in case that turns out to be the case, and let me assure you that it was never my intention to cause any such offence. This book has been written out of love for the Caucasus, and not for any other reason.

Geopolitically, the Caucasus "is the pivot about which everything sways: American economic interests, Russian territorial interests, Islamic religious interests, all factors in the oscillating local politics" (Griffin, 2001, p.3). Moreover, this situation is in a sense nothing new, for it was considered just as critical 150 years ago, albeit for different reasons.

As to why the region it is now proving to be such a focus of interest, whatever excuses might be given for the political decisions that have been taken and the military action that has been initiated, the main reason of course is economic – oil to be more precise – the estimated 100 billion barrels of crude oil in the Caspian Sea, now being piped from Azerbaijan through Georgia, and then on through Turkey to the west. And anyone who has spent time in the region will know from experience that religious conflict hardly enters into the equation. For the fact of the matter is that most peoples have little difficulty in co-existing peacefully with each other on a personal level whatever their beliefs might be.

Another claim made about the region is that

> Everything shifts in the Caucasus, blown by some of the strongest winds on earth. Even the ground moves, splintered by fault lines. In early Georgian myths, it is said that when the mountains were young, they had legs – could walk from the edges of the oceans to the deserts, flirting with the low hills, shrouding them with soft clouds of love (Griffin, 2001, p.2).

But what about those aspects of life which remain relatively constant – the traditional practices of the mountain people, the practices that are reflected in their folk-tales and their folklore? It is these constants that this study concentrates on, in particular those that relate to shamanism.

> The search for national character is no more than a kind of nineteenth-century-after-dinner pastime. The search to identify a patronizing stereotype unravels as an attempt to gratify our own superiority and brilliantly subtle capacity at categorizing other peoples; an activity which we hardly notice borders on the racist. Maybe the most one can say is that there are certain "sides" to a national character, or that a certain amount of statistical clumping occurs around certain activities. No other

significant conclusions can be drawn (Walker, 1997, p.v.).

And if this applies to the search for national character, then what applies to the search for the character of a region consisting of a number of independent countries and numerous peoples? Clearly it is an impossible task, which is why the present author will not make the mistake of attempting it. Instead, each country will have an independent chapter devoted to it in this volume.

In what way the category "religion" is applicable to the study of ancient cultures is a question of great interest to scholars. However, whether it is or not is in a sense irrelevant to this work. What is needed here is a term to refer to the subject matter focused on, and in the absence of any more suitable and generally accepted alternative, the term "religion" best satisfies this requirement. Shamanism will therefore be classified as a religion, but as "a mystical religion of ritual observance" for the reasons that follow.

It is customary for religions to involve some sort of ritual observance, such as the sacraments of Christianity, the five daily prayers facing Mecca of Islam, or the elaborate rituals of Tibetan Buddhism. Indeed, as Gray (2004) points out, a strong case can be made for the fact that the heart of spiritual life is not to be found in doctrine but lies in practice – in ritual, observance and sometimes even mystical experience. If we consider some of the major religions, for example, nothing as simple as a creed can be extracted from the complex practices of Hinduism, Buddhism has never attached importance to doctrine, and in Judaism priority is given to practice rather than belief and this applies to some Sufi traditions too. The phrase "a religion of ritual observance" has been used in particular to describe Shinto – "a religion not of theology but of ritual observance" (Driver, 1991, p.38) – but the same description, for the same reasons, can be applied to shamanism too.

Other religions, apart from Shinto, can also be listed under this heading, Wicca for example. As in the case of Shinto, there is no one bible or prayer book in Wicca and the primary concern is not ethics, dogma, or theology. Rather, it is a religion of ritual practice. These practices include marking eight holiday "sabbats" in the "wheel of the year", falling on the solstices, equinoxes and the four "cross-quarter days" on or about the first of February, May, August and November. Many Wiccans also mark "esbats," rituals for worship in accordance with a given moon phase (such as the night of the full moon).

The Australian Aborigines can be said to practise a religion of ritual observance too as James Cowan expressively conveys: "[T]he Aborigines have made the "face of the earth" their Bhagavad Gita, their Torah, their Bible or Koran. Indeed the Dreaming is the Aboriginal Ark of the Covenant which they have been carrying about the Australian continent since the beginning of time" (Cowan, 1992, pp.2-3).

As for including the word "mystical" in the definition, it was decided to do so in view of the fact that shamans "are separated from the rest of the community by the intensity of their own religious experience" in the same way as "monks, mystics, and saints within Christian churches" are (Eliade, 1964, p.8). Another reason for including the adjective is that "A unique characteristic of mysticism ... is the denial of the languages' ability to express religious truth ... [with mystics claiming] that truth lies beyond any possibility of expression by terms derived from sensual experience or logical deduction" (Dan, 2006, p.9). And this is a view that the majority of shamanic practitioners would undoubtedly share.

Even before the Soviets, the Caucasus

> was a land of myths and tales as tall as the peaks themselves ... In Armenia, Noah's Ark lies on the borders. In Azerbaijan, the Garden of Eden is said to lurk somewhere in the south. Georgia is not to be outdone. If her neighbours boast of the genesis of man, Georgia claims to have been home to the gods. Prometheus was bound to one of her great peaks, his liver torn

daily by the circling birds of prey (Griffin, 2001, p.2).

It should therefore come as no surprise that the region not only contains a rich source of traditional tales, but that the stories are the products of so many different influences – including pagan, Christian and Islamic – in view of the troubled history of the land. However, as it is the shamanic influences that we are primarily interested in here, and that will form the focus of this work, let us start by defining what we mean by shamanism and the shamanic story before we venture any further.

For the purposes of this study, a shaman is understood to be someone who performs an ecstatic (in a trance state), imitative, or demonstrative ritual of a séance (or a combination of all three), at will (in other words, whenever he or she chooses to do so), in which aid is sought from beings in (what are considered to be) other realities generally for healing purposes or for divination – both for individuals and/or the community. What this suggests is that Eliade's focus on the journey as the defining feature of shamanism is not a true reflection of what actually takes place, at least not in the case of the demonstrative and imitative forms.

As for the practice of shamanism, it is understood to encompass a personalistic view of the world, in which life is seen to be not only about beliefs and practices, but also about relationships – how we are related, and how we relate to each other. And when this breaks down – in other words, when it is not taking place in a harmonious and constructive way – the shaman, employing what Graham Harvey likes to refer to as "adjusted styles of communication", makes it his or her business to resolve such issues.

> In shamanism [the notion of interdependence] is the idea of the kinship of all life, the recognition that nothing can exist in and of itself without being in relationship to other things, and therefore that it is insane for us to consider ourselves as essentially unrelated parts of the whole Earth (Halifax in

> Nicholson, (comp.), 1987, p.220).

And through neurotheology, this assertion so often heard expressed in neo-shamanic circles that all life is connected, can now be substantiated:

> Through the new medical discipline of neurotheology developed largely at the Massachusetts Institute of Technology, it has been shown that during mystical ecstasy (or its equivalent, entheogenic shamanic states [states induced by ingesting hallucinogens]), the individual experiences a blurring of the boundaries on the ego and feels at "one with Nature"; the ego is no longer confined within the body, but extends outward to all of Nature; other living beings come to share in the ego, as an authentic communion with the total environment, which is sensed as in some way divine (Ruck, Staples, et al., 2007, p.76).

The peculiar interconnectedness of communities through ties of family and obligation found in the Caucasus would suggest that this is a concept that its peoples are more than familiar with. The interconnectedness often takes the form of clan networks, traditionally an important element of Caucasus society, both north and south of the mountains.

> Circassian families were organized into groups composed of a number of households all stemming from a single, often mythical, progenitor. In Chechen and Ingush regions several extended families could be tied together into a single *teip*, a broad collection of people with links to a particular village or district. In Dagestan multiple villages were sometimes grouped together into distinct *jamaats*, headed by a council of elders. In Georgia clan relationships might run along regional or subethnic lines, such as Mingrelians from the Abkhaz borderlands or Gurians from western Georgia (King, 2008, pp.202-203).

Rather than being a product of Soviet rule, the sharing or pooling of resources and wealth has long been practised by the people. It has also served to sustain them through all the hardships they have had to endure.

What we can see from this is that shamanism, albeit under different names, and in various forms, has thrived for millennia; and it has to be said that it is hard to imagine a tradition surviving for so long in so many cultures unless there were effective components to it (see Walsh, 2007, pp.120).

> In Marxist anthropological theory, shamanism represented one of the early forms of religion that later gave rise to more sophisticated beliefs in the course of human advancement, a view that Marxism incorporated from its predecessor – social evolutionism. The premise of Marxism was that eventually, at the highest levels of civilization, the sacred and religion would eventually die out (Znamenski, 2007, p.322).

Though history has of course since disproved this, the theory clearly had a great bearing on what was written in the former Soviet Union about shamanism, and also on people's attitudes in the former Soviet Republics towards such practices.

On the other hand, it has been suggested that "all intellectuals driven by nationalist sentiments directly or indirectly are always preoccupied with searching for the most ancient roots of their budding nations in order to ground their compatriots in particular soil and to make them more indigenous" (Znamenski, 2007, p.28). Although this might apply to searching for the roots of Christianity or Islam, when it comes to searching for the roots of pagan practices, interest on the part of the people, at least in my experience, has not been so forthcoming. This impasse, coupled with the effects of the repressions against religions, including shamanism, unleashed by the Soviet government between the 1930s and 1950s, along with the recent surge of interest in both

Orthodox Christianity and Islam, a backlash to the seventy years of officially sanctioned atheism, makes research into the subject no easy business. Indeed, some have even suggested that the paganism of the ancient inhabitants of the land is almost entirely inaccessible to us. Be this as it may, the fact that a task is difficult is no reason for not attempting it, and this study will at least help to set the process in motion.

Even when there are no written records, religious activities leave behind vestiges and artefacts allow the reconstruction of the world-view of the past. However, what happens when such archaeological evidence is limited or even in some cases non-existent? Then all we really have to turn to are the folktales still told by the descendents of the ancient peoples, and from them we can make some educated guesses as to what the world-view once was, which is what this study sets out to do.

Hunt (2006) points out in his article 'Colour Symbolism in the Folk Literature of the Caucasus', that almost the entire culture of the indigenous population of the Caucasus, apart from the low-lying parts of Georgia, was oral until the early 1920s. He goes on to add that

> Between around 1860 and 1920, before writing was developed for most of the mountain tribes, this oral literature was extensively recorded. These records cannot therefore be dismissed as just the stories of ignorant peasants, but were the "classical literature" and the entire actual culture of these people, who had committed it to memory rather than being able to record it in writing.

Dirr, who compiled a collection of folktales from the region, came to the conclusion that "by studying the mythological ideas and beliefs of the Caucasus peoples [that one can read about in the literature Hunt refers to above] one cannot avoid the thought that there used to exist in the Caucasus one religion, which was subsequently obscured ..." (Dirr 1915, p. 13-16). And, as we shall see, that one religion could well have been shamanism.

Before proceeding any further, we should perhaps pause at this point to consider what the process of an outsider trying to understand narratives that are representative of another culture actually entails, as this is precisely what the author of this particular volume is attempting to do. As such an outsider does not share the cultural knowledge of the peoples

> whose narratives he or she is considering, this also means that he does not know what world the narratives refer to. Nor does he know the ways of telling about this world. He lacks 1) the ability to perceive knowledge of the world in the manner of the [members of that other culture] … 2) an understanding of how the [members of that other culture] … organize this knowledge into a narrative, and 3) an understanding of how the information in the narrative should be interpreted (Siikala, 1992, p.204).

Moreover, none of these problems that the Westerner faces can be fully solved by background reading, however extensive such reading might be. On the other hand, as an outsider, the Westerner can see the narrative with a new pair of eyes, and thus appreciate aspects to it that the insider might not perhaps consider or that the insider merely takes for granted and glosses over. And for this reason, though fraught with obvious difficulties, the outsider's attempt to understand and to present appreciations of such narratives is still an enterprise that is more than worth undertaking and one that can, without a doubt, pay rich dividends, as hopefully this study will show.

***

Oliver and Marjory Wardrop were born into a Victorian society of empire and adventure. In their lives the brother and sister would develop a refined friendship not only between themselves, but also with the people of a whole country – Georgia. Their example to the Victorian age of exploration was to discover a nation from its centre outwards, via its literature – for which they would receive the Georgian peoples' affection long after their deaths. After Oliver's first visit to Georgia in 1887 and the publication of his book 'The Kingdom of Georgia,' brother and sister painstakingly taught themselves the language, then began translating Georgia's folktales and poetry into English. Their scholarship would provide Britain with a solid platform for the ensuing political and economic relationship, and a focus of trust for the Georgian people.

The importance of this cultural grounding to a political role was acknowledged in 1919, when the Foreign Secretary, Lord Curzon, invited Oliver to become the first Chief British Commissioner of Transcaucasia – a post he held until just before the Bolshevik invasion of 1921.

Today the legacy of Oliver and Marjory remains as strong as ever. Marjory Wardrop's first English translation of Shola Rustaveli's 12th century masterpiece 'The Man in the Panther's Skin' is still regarded among international scholars, as is the Marjory Wardrop Fund at Oxford University created by Oliver after Marjory's death in 1909. The Bodleian Library's Wardrop Collection of books and manuscripts remains one of the finest collections of Kartvelian material outside Georgia (Naysmith, 1989, p.4).

This book, in a sense, is an attempt to follow in the Wardrops' footsteps, to discover the Caucasus from its centre outwards, but in particular the pagan roots of the peoples, and to do so via their folktales. As to how far it succeeds in its intentions – that is for you, the reader, to say.

Chapter 1

The Shamanic Story: What is it, and why do we need it?

In her paper "South Siberian and Central Asian Hero Tales and Shamanistic Rituals", the Leipzig researcher Erika Taube suggests that

> Folktales – being expressions of early stages of the development of human society – reflect reality: material culture, social relations, customs, [and] religious beliefs. When folktales were being formed and appeared as vivid forms of spiritual and artistic expression in correspondence with the general social development, those elements, which nowadays are usually regarded as fantastic creations of the human mind, were strictly believed phenomena, i.e. they were accepted as facts. Therefore, it is not at all a new idea that such tales sometimes reflect shamanistic beliefs and conceptions (Taube, 1984, p. 344).

If they were forms of "artistic expression", however, then they could well have been regarded as such by those they were told to and we actually have no way of knowing whether they were "accepted as facts" or not. On the other hand, what we can show is that they do reflect shamanistic beliefs and conceptions, and this becomes apparent once we start to analyze them.

Sir James Frazer made a similar claim in his abridged version of *The Golden Bough*, first published in 1922: "folk-tales are a faithful reflection of the world as it appeared to the primitive mind; and that we may be sure that any idea which commonly occurs in them, however absurd it may seem to us, must once have been an ordinary article of belief" (Frazer, 1993, p.668). In reality, however, there is no way we can be certain that any idea that appears in such tales must once have been an ordinary article of belief as, not being able to get inside other people's minds, we cannot possibly know what was actually the case.

On the other hand, as Emily Lyle (2007) points out in the abstract to her paper "Narrative Form and the Structure of Myth", what we can be reasonably sure of is that "At each stage in transmission of a tale from generation to generation, modifications take place but something remains. Thus there is a potential for material to be retained from a time in the distant past when the narrative was embedded in a total oral worldview or cosmology." In view of the fact that in the past shamanism was widely practiced in the regions where the tales in this study were told, it is therefore highly likely that a shamanic worldview and shamanic cosmology is to be found embedded in them.

Stories have traditionally been classified as epics, myths, sagas, legends, folk tales, fairy tales, parables or fables. However, the definitions of the terms have a tendency to overlap (see Berman, 2006, p.150-152), making it difficult to classify and categorize material. Another problem with the traditional terminology is that the genre system formed on the basis of European folklore cannot be fully applied universally.

Consider, for example, Eliade's definition of myth. For Eliade the characteristics of myth, as experienced by archaic societies, are that it constitutes the absolutely true and sacred History of the acts of the Supernaturals, which is always related to a "creation", which leads to a knowledge, experienced ritually, of the origin of things and thus the ability to control them, and which is "lived" in the sense that one is profoundly affected by the power of the events it recreates (see Eliade, 1964, pp.18-19). However, many stories are "lived" in the sense that one is profoundly affected by the events they recreate without them necessarily being myths. Moreover, many shamanic stories could be regarded as having the above characteristics but would still not necessarily be classified as myths.

Another problem encountered is that a number of the definitions of what a myth is are so general in nature that they tend to be of little value. For example, the suggestion that a myth is "a story about something significant [that] ... can take place in the past ... or in the present, or in the future" (Segal, 2004, p.5) really does not help us at all as this could be applied to more or less every type of tale.

Mary Beard, considering the significance of distinctions between such categories as "myth," "legend," and "folk-tale", concludes that in fact no technical definition distinguishing these is wholly plausible, since matters of technical definition are not really the issue. "For these are value judgments masquerading as professional jargon; they are justifications of neglect – the dustbin categories for all kinds of mythic thinking that we would rather not treat as 'myth'" (see Winterbourne, 2007, p.15). Be this as it may, it is surely indisputable that we need some form of labeling for the categories in order to be able to refer to them, and the argument being presented in this study is that the time has come to revise these categories.

For this reason a case was argued in Berman (2006) for the introduction of a new genre, termed the shamanic story. This can be defined as a story that has either been based on or inspired by a shamanic journey, or one that contains a number of the elements typical of such a journey. Like other genres, it has "its own style, goals, entelechy, rhetoric, developmental pattern, and characteristic roles" (Turner, 1985, p.187), and like other genres it can be seen to differ to a certain extent from culture to culture. It should perhaps be noted at this point, however, that there are both emic and etic ways of regarding narrative (see Turner, 1982, p.65) and the term "shamanic story" clearly presents an outside view. It should also be pointed out that what is being offered here is a polytheistic definition of what the shamanic story is, in which a pool of characteristics can apply, but need not.

Characteristics typical of the genre include the way in which the stories all tend to contain embedded texts (often the account of the shamanic journey itself), how the number of actors is clearly limited as one would expect in subjective accounts of what can be regarded as inner journeys, and how the stories tend to be used for healing purposes.

The healing effect of such stories derives from their dramatic potential to induce a psychological effect – the way in which they can free the reader from a debilitating self-image by focusing on his / her consciousness instead on a world of supernatural power. Additionally, through the use of narrative, shamans are able to provide their patients "with a language, by means of which unexpressed, and otherwise inexpressible, psychic states can be expressed" (Lévi-Strauss, 1968, p.198).

In his Foreword to *Tales of the Sacred and the Supernatural,* Eliade admits to repeatedly taking up "the themes of *sortie du temps,* or temporal dislocation, and of the alteration or the transmutation of space" (Eliade, 1981, p.10), and these are themes that appear over and over again in shamanic stories too.

They are also frequently examples of what Jürgen Kremer, transpersonal psychologist and spiritual practitioner, called "tales of power" after one of Carlos Castaneda's novels. He defines such texts as conscious verbal constructions based on numinous experiences in non-ordinary reality, "which guide individuals and help them to integrate the spiritual, mythical, or archetypal aspects of their internal and external experience in unique, meaningful, and fulfilling ways" (Kremer, 1988, p.192). In other words, they are teaching tales.

The style of storytelling most frequently employed in both shamanic stories and in fairy tales is that of magic realism, in which although "the point of departure is 'realistic' (recognizable events in chronological succession, everyday atmosphere, verisimilitude, characters with more or less predictable psychological reactions), … soon strange discontinuities or gaps appear in the 'normal,' true-to-life texture of the narrative" (Calinescu, 1978, p.386). In other words, what happens is that our expectations based on our intuitive knowledge of physics are ultimately breached and knocked out.

Magic realism can be described as consisting of "a fusion of logic and nonsense. It can be seen as a foretaste of the changing world conditions, in which our minds, having mastered 'black and white' – or normal earthbound logic, must now begin to operate beyond the threshold of purely sense-based thinking to master a different, higher logic" (Hallam, 2002, p.48). Though it might be better to replace the term "sense-based thinking" with "logical thinking" here, and though it is debatable whether or not it is necessarily "higher", what cannot be denied is that it is certainly a different way of operating, which is of course a large part of its attraction. For it gives us new options to work with.

Parallels can be drawn between shamanic rituals and shamanic stories. Given that the stories are often based on accounts of shamanic journeys, this should come as no surprise. And the three phases of separation, transition, and incorporation, which van Gennep (1909/1977) identified in rites of passage, can be found in shamanic stories too.

> Turner (1982) investigates the characteristics of the phase of transition or liminal phase which is clearly demarcated from profane space and time. Through specific rites that must be performed a cultural realm that is defined as "out of time," i.e., beyond or outside time that measures secular processes and routines, is constructed. During the liminal phase the ritual subjects pass through a period and area of ambiguity which has few of the attributes of either the preceding or subsequent profane states and, may also include subversive and ludic (or playful) events ... The cognitive patterns that create order and meaning in everyday life are no longer applicable in the liminal phase (Turner 1982). ... The liminal phase of the ritual – allows for playful mixing events, feelings, thoughts and fantasies

> beyond the everyday order of space and time (Eigner, 2008, pp.34-35).

With magic realism what happens is that the expectations we have based on our intuitive knowledge of physics which apply at the outset are breached and knocked out in the liminal stage before the *status quo* is restored in the resolution. And the agent responsible for restoring equilibrium to the community in the incorporation phase is invariably the "shaman" character.

When magic is used in such tales, it is done so chiefly as an instrument – the means by which an impossible task is accomplished, for example – and frequently the search for a magical object serves as a hero task, such as the need to discover the external soul of the villain and thus put an end to him or her (see Hoogasian-Villa, 1966, p.54). Magic realism characterizes the style of storytelling in all of the tales in this study.

"Liminality, marginality and structural inferiority are conditions in which are frequently generated myths, symbols, rituals, philosophical systems, and works of art" (Turner, 1995, pp.128-9). And this applies to shamanic stories too. It is during the liminal stage referred to by Turner that the shaman undertakes the "journey" and the account of the experience then follows. Turner sees this stage as a movement from structure to anti-structure. However, it can in fact be argued that the liminal stage has a structure of its own, just as the "journey" which takes place during the liminal stage does.

The shaman's journey is followed by his / her account of the experience – the story of the ascent to the Upper World or the decent to the world below, how the spirits encountered along the way were dealt with, and how the return was achieved. And as Eliade noted, "Probably a large number of epic 'subjects' or motifs, as well as many characters, images, and clichés of epic literature ... were borrowed from the narratives of shamans describing their journeys and adventures in the superhuman worlds" (Eliade, 1989, p.510). Evidence to support this claim can be found in the biblical story of Jonah, for example (see Berman, 2007), which can be interpreted as a spiritual journey to the Lower World, or the ascent to the Upper World in the fairy-tale *Jack and the Beanstalk.* A cosmology serves to orient a community to its world by defining the place of its people in the universal scheme of things. It tells the members of the community who they are and where they stand in relation to the rest of creation (see Mathews, 1994, p.12). Such cosmologies are presented in the stories that are told by shamans in that they account for the origin and nature of the world and so help us to make sense of it. Moreover, the telling of such tales by the shaman confirms his / her mastery of the skills required to deal with the spirits and inspires the community's confidence in his / her abilities to act on their behalf.

Entering the ritual space or the core of a shamanic story can be compared to entering a temple because it serves as a focusing lens. When we enter marked-off space, everything – at least potentially – assumes significance, and even the ordinary becomes sacred by having our attention directed to it in a special way (see Smith, 1982, pp.54-55).

It has been suggested that

> Once we are acquitted of our ritual duties, we re-enter profane life with more courage and enthusiasm, not only because we have put ourselves in touch with a higher source of energy, but also because our forces have been reinvigorated by living briefly a life that is more relaxed, more free and easy. In this way, religion has a charm that is not the least of its attractions (Durkheim, 2001, p.285).

What is being proposed here is that listening to a powerful shamanic story can have a similar effect too, with "the proof of the pudding being in the eating".

> Skeptics will argue that it is impossible to eliminate from analysis the Christian [or Islamic] influence on what sources there are available to us, such that we can never be certain in any one case that we are indeed dealing with beliefs that are authentically pagan. This view is now so widely held that we can in justice think of it as the prevailing orthodoxy (Winterbourne, 2007, p.24).

And the same argument could be applied to the attempt to ascertain whether we are dealing with beliefs that are authentically shamanic in any of the tales in this volume. Nevertheless, just because a task is difficult is no reason for not attempting it. If it were, then no progress would ever be made in any research that we might be involved in. For this reason, despite whatever the prevailing orthodoxy might be, there is surely every reason to conduct such a study as this.

Before concluding this chapter, it is worth making two further observations on the nature of the tales included in this study.

> Since shamanism is so widespread, it is self-evident that the tales about shamans [and shamanic stories as defined in this volume] will be coloured by the narrative traits and modes of cultural expression specific to the various regions (Hultkrantz, 1993, p.41).

Additionally, it should be noted that "In areas where shamanism has long been a thing of the past, many tales contain only vague, piecemeal or inaccurate recollections of shamans and their like" (Hultkrantz, 1993, p.51). On the other hand, however vague, piecemeal or inaccurate these recollections might be, this does not invalidate the classification of the tales they are embedded in as shamanic stories for the purposes of this study, or their value. In fact, just the reverse is the case, as in the absence of more concrete evidence, they may well help us to reconstruct how things used to be in a time when shamanism was prevalent in the region.

> According to the finest traditions of storytelling, there are only a set number of archetypal story lines to draw upon and all of them relate to the human condition - to the struggle of becoming fully human. The heroes, or heroines, find themselves facing impossible conditions that can only be overcome by an initiation journey, during which the outer struggle is seen as symbolic of an inner struggle, and when this is won the outer dangers fall away (Hallam, 2002, p.47).

For the shaman, however, the outer struggle is perceived to be as real as the inner struggle, simply another form of reality, and the shamanic story is an account of just such a journey. The chapters that follow present selected examples of these tales and notes on the countries they come from.

Chapter 2

Armenia

> If the Scriptures are rightly understood, it was in Armenia that Paradise was placed – Armenia, which has paid as dearly as the descendents of Adam for that fleeting participation of its soil in the happiness of him who was created from its dust. It was in Armenia that the flood first abated, and the dove alighted. But with the disappearance of Paradise itself may be dated almost the unhappiness of the country; for though long a powerful kingdom, it was scarcely ever an independent one, and the satraps of Persia and the pachas of Turkey have alike desolated the region where God created man in his own image (taken from Byron, *Letters and Journals*, Leslie Marchand (ed.), London, 1976, vol. V, p.157).

What can we say about Armenia? "There is no other country like her. She has played a unique and perhaps indispensable role as a buffer between Asia and Europe, a mediator between two seemingly irreconcilable civilizations and ways of life. And her dark beauty is eternal" (Surmelian, 1968, pp.23-24).

Located in the southern Caucasus, Armenia is the smallest of the former Soviet republics, and is bounded by Georgia in the north, Azerbaijan in the east, Iran in the south, and Turkey in the west. Frequently referred to as one of the cradles of civilization, it is also considered by many to have been the first country in the world to officially embrace Christianity as its religion (c. 300).

Armenia, like neighboring Georgia, is in a region which is a crossroads between Asia and Europe, and has more often than not been conquered by the dominant regional power of the day, starting with the Assyrians, Babylonians, Persians, Macedonians, through to the Ottomans and finally the Russians. As a result, an Armenian diaspora has thus existed more or less throughout the nation's history, with emigration having been particularly heavy since independence. So much so, that an estimated 60% of the total eight million Armenians worldwide now live outside the country. Nevertheless, once again like Georgia, the country has managed to hold onto a unique cultural and linguistic identity which is reflected in its folklore.

As a consequence of Soviet era policies, the number of active religious practitioners in the country is relatively low, but the link between Armenian ethnicity and the Armenian Church is strong. An estimated 90 percent of citizens nominally belong to the Armenian Church, an independent Eastern Christian denomination with its spiritual centre at the Etchmiadzin cathedral and monastery.

It is all too easy these days to paint a totally negative picture of life under Soviet communism, especially when it comes to the matter of religious freedom, but in the case of Armenia it would be an injustice to do so for

> Soviet communism protected the Armenian people from Turkism ... Moreover, despite its internationalist posture, communism built up a nation in Soviet Armenia from individuals and groups of widely differing geographical origins. The power to withstand, and the sense of nationhood, have to be balanced against the totalitarianism and Stalinism which were part of the state ideology, although less visible at the start (Walker, 1997, p.140).

As for the current status of religious freedom, although the Armenian Constitution as amended in December 2005 provides for freedom of religion, the reality of the situation is that the Armenian (Apostolic) Church, which has formal legal status as the national church, enjoys some privileges not available to other religious groups. Societal attitudes towards some minority religious groups appear to be somewhat ambivalent too, with reports of societal discrimination directed against members of these groups.

Only registered groups may publish newspapers or magazines, rent meeting places, broadcast programs on television or radio, or officially sponsor the visas of visitors, although there is no prohibition on individual members doing so. And to qualify for registration, religious organizations must "be free from materialism and of a purely spiritual nature," and must subscribe to a doctrine based on "historically recognized holy scriptures." In the case of religions based on ritual observance rather than "holy scriptures" though, were an application for registration made, it is unclear what scriptures could be presented to the Office of the State Registrar to satisfy such a requirement.

We find what is now Armenia referred to in the Old Testament, with the Book of Genesis relating

> how Noah's Ark, as the waters of the flood subsided, came to rest, not "on Mount Ararat" as is commonly misstated – the Armenians call this *Mount Masis*, a name (*Masios*) used by Greek geographers to denote a range to the south-west – but "upon the mountains of (the land of) Ararat", i.e. a country known to the ancient Assyrians as *Urartu* (Downing, 1972, p. ix).

The region of Ararat was then invaded by the Armenians after the Urartian kingdom, plagued by Assyrian and Cimmerian attacks, fell to the Medes in 612 B.C. The most momentous event in the national life of Armenia, however, and the event which was the chief determining factor in the early history of the country, was the change of religion made by the adoption of Christianity, which was finally established by Tiridates (A.D. 286-342).

> By this the Armenians were entirely severed from the pagan Persians and brought into close contact with the Greeks, whose representative was then the Emperor of Byzantium. As a result of this religious agreement, a treaty was concluded in 319 between Tiridates and Constantine, the first Christian Emperor of Rome, by which the two Christian monarchs bound themselves to defend each other against all pagans.
>
> The adoption of Christianity meant, to the Armenians, a revolution in their whole view of life, a severance from their ancestral beliefs, though these beliefs have left traces in Armenian folklore which are visible even to this day. These beliefs and the folklore arising out of them were regarded by the Christian clergy as a poisonous flower grown up in the fields of paganism. The historians of the period have chronicled the efforts of the clergy to exterminate every relic of the old faith. Temples were pulled down and churches built in their stead; images and other monuments were broken in pieces; heathen books and records were destroyed; pagan festivals were turned into Christian ones. We learn from Faustus of Byzantium that laws were even made against the use and the singing of pagan songs (Boyajian, 1916, p. 151).

Nevertheless, despite the fact that the Roman Catholic and Orthodox Christian Churches took the place of the old religions in Europe and across western Eurasia, this applied mainly to the urban centers.

> Beyond the borders of Rome's control, in the most northern and eastern fringes and on the western isles, and in the rural environments amongst the "country folk" or *pagani*, the old religions continued, pejoratively designated after them as Paganism. Even when officially Christianized, the religion of the Pagans remained an assimilation, merely an overlay of the newer cults, or it passed unnoticed under other names, with its

> myths and beliefs adapting and surviving primarily in less objectionable forms such as folktales and bizarre or quaint festival rites (Ruck, Staples, et al., 2007, p.3).

And this is very much what occurred in the case of Armenian paganism too. Not only can reminders be found in the traditional dances, songs, and rites still being performed, but also in the folktales still being told. Even after so many centuries of Christianity in Armenia, elements of paganism live on in the country to this day. Moreover, the origins of Armenian paganism could well date back even further into the distant past, when shamanism would have been practiced in the land.

Their concept of the soul, for example, would indicate that this was likely – the belief that departed bad souls could pursue the living, resulting in their soul loss:

> Since it was believed that the soul left the mouth in death, it lived on apart from the body and was invisible. It could assume physical shape somewhat smaller than the body, or an animal shape, the most important of which was a bird ... Even inanimate objects, such as trees, were associated with soul beliefs, and the poor health of a tree symbolized that the human owner was in danger, too.

Departed souls could appear as good or evil. Good ghosts were associated with angels and holy beings; bad ghosts were considered to be the souls of sinners ... In the shape of animals or men these unclean souls appeared before men and brought misfortune to them. Such departed bad souls constantly pursued the living and were eager to take them along. To prevent this, the living flattered the dead with attention and honored them with a funeral. They provided a *hokeh-hatz* [funeral dinner] with abundant food for the mourners. If, however, flattery was ineffective, the evil force of the soul might be destroyed by eating part of the dead man's heart, which was, and still is, considered the seat of the soul.

> ... The belief that the soul of the departed needs special care exists even today. Special prayers for the peace of the departed are still said in church and until recently were chanted in individual homes on Saturday nights over the faint glow of incense. On the Monday after Easter the great celebration of *Merelotz* [Memorial Day] occurs. In Armenia whole families spent the afternoon at the cemeteries of their departed (Hoogasian-Villa, 1966, p.61).

As for the folktales, they can be divided "into wonder tales ... and realistic tales of everyday life ... although this is a rough distinction at best for there are wonder tales with realistic elements in them, and realistic tales not altogether devoid of the marvellous" (Surmelian, 1968, p.11). The tale presented here is of the former type.

Epithets are frequently used in the stories. In *The Girl who changed into a Boy*, there are the examples of "the King's daughter" and "the old woman's daughter". We never learn their names, only the name of the horse.

> Another feature we find is that formulas are repeated, a popular one being "Whether they travelled a long or short time, only God knows." Frequently, the following disclaimer appears too: "Whether it happened or not ..." or "there was and there wasn't..." As for the story endings, many are a variation on ... "Three apples fell from heaven – one apple for the storyteller, the second for the person listening to the story, and the third for the whole, wide world." Another common ending formula is "They attained their happiness. May you attain your happiness, too" (see Marshall, 2007, p.xxviii).

A comprehensive introduction by Aram Raffi to the religious beliefs and practices that prevailed in Armenia in pre-Christian times can be found in *Armenian Legends and Poems* and, as a starting point, it is presented below:

> The principal god of Armenia was *Aramazd,* whom the Armenians called "the Architect of the Universe, Creator of Heaven and Earth." He was also the father of the other gods. The Armenians annually celebrated the festival of this god on the 1st day of Navasard [which, according to the later calendar of pagan Armenia, was in August], when they sacrificed white animals of various kinds – goats, horses, mules, with whose blood they filled goblets of gold and silver. The most prominent sanctuaries of Aramazd were in the ancient city of Ani in Daranali, the burial-place of the Armenian kings, as well as in the village of Bagavan in Bagravand. Aramazd had an attendant incorporeal spirit, named *Tir* or *Grogh* ("writer"), whom he sent to earth to watch men and record in a book their good and evil deeds. After death, human souls were conducted by Tir to Aramazd, who opened the book at each soul's record, in accordance with which he assigned a reward or punishment. In a village near Vargharshapat there was a temple of this god, where the priests interpreted dreams after consulting his oracle. The influence of Tir was great in Armenia, for he was a personification of hope and fear. There are traces of the cult of this god in the Armenian language. It is still usual to hear, used as a curse, the expression, "May Grogh take you!" The son of Aramazd was *Mihr,* Fire. He guided the heroes in battle and conferred wreaths on the victors. The word *mehian* ("temple") is derived from Mihr; also some Christian names. One of the months in the ancient Armenian calendar (Mehekan) was named after him. His commemoration-day was celebrated with … great splendour at the beginning of spring. Fires were kindled in the open market-place in his honour, and a lantern lighted from one of these fires was kept burning in his temple throughout the year. This custom of kindling fires in the spring

is still observed in some parts of Armenia.

Although the Persians and the Armenians were both worshippers of Mihr, the conceptions and observances of the two nations differed. The Armenian sacred fire was invisible, but the Persian was material and was kept up in all the temples. For this reason the Armenians called the Persians fire-worshippers. But the Armenians had also a visible fire-god, who, although material, was intangible – the sun – to which many temples were dedicated and after which one of the months (*Areg*) was named. Long after the introduction of Christianity, there was a sect of sunworshippers existent in Armenia, who were called "Children of the Sun." A small remnant of them is still supposed to be found, dwelling between the Tigris and the Euphrates. Traces of sun-worship are also evident in the Armenian language and in the Armenian literature of Christian times. Some sayings and phrases are still in use which contain references to sun-worship, such as the expression of endearment, "Let me die for your sun!" and the oath, "Let the sun of my son be witness."

One of the most famous Armenian goddesses was *Anahit*, who answered to the Greek Artemis and the Roman Diana. She was a " pure and spotless goddess," and, as a daughter of Aramazd, was "mother of chastity," as well as the benefactress of the whole human race; "through her the Armenian land exists, from her it draws its life; she is the glory of our nation and its protectress"; and for her the ancient Armenians felt intense love and adoration.

Many images and shrines were dedicated to her under the names of "the Golden Mother," "the Being of Golden Birth," etc. Every summer there was a festival in her honour. On that day, a dove and a rose were offered to her golden image, whence the day was called *Vardavar*, which means "the flaming of the Rose." On the introduction of Christianity, the temple of Anahit was destroyed and her festival became the Feast of the

Transfiguration of Christ; it falls in the last days of the year according to the ancient Armenian calendar; but the name "Vardavar" still remains and doves are still set flying on that day.

The sister of Anahit was *Astghik* [which means "little star" in Armenian], the goddess of beauty, a personification of the moon, corresponding to the Phoenician and Sidonian Astarte. Strange to say, the Persians had no goddess of beauty, but the bright sky of Armenia, its numerous valleys, the torrents running down from snow-capped mountains, the lakes, the cultivated fields and meadows tended to strengthen the sense of beauty, and, therefore, Armenia had a goddess of beauty, who was not to be found in the pantheon of the neighbouring country.

The Armenians assigned Astghik a husband worthy of her. He was Vahagn, deified on account of his valour. In ancient songs, he is credited with a miraculous birth. The fires of heaven and earth, and the sea crimson in the light of dawn, travailed to bring him into being. ... Vahagn was called Vishapakagh (Uprooter of dragons), as he cleared the Armenian land of monsters and saved it from evil influences. His exploits were known not only in Armenia, but in the abode of the gods. Having stolen corn from the barns of King Barsham of Assyria, he ran away and tried to hide himself in heaven. From the ears he dropped arose the Milky Way, which is called in Armenia the Track of the Corn-stealer.

The third daughter of Aramazd was *Nané* or *Nooné*. She was the goddess of contrivance. It was believed by the Armenians that contrivance was a necessary power for a woman, because, in the management of the household, she had to make big things out of small ones, and circumstances were already against her on account of the vicissitudes which Armenia was constantly undergoing.

Sandaramet, the wife of Aramazd, was an invisible goddess

and a personification of the earth. Aramazd sent rain upon her, which brought forth the vegetation on the earth. She came to be a synonym of Hades and was very frequently referred to as such in theological books and in the hymnary of the Christian Church.

Besides these gods of their own, the Armenians also adopted alien divinities. When Tigranes brought a number of Phoenicians to Armenia as prisoners, they brought with them their god Ammon, from whose name [some say] comes the word *Ammonor*, "the day of Ammon" – the New Year. Assyrian, Arab, and other emigrations also led to the introduction of foreign deities. An Armenian king, when he brought home captives, also introduced the gods of those captives, whose images were placed in the temples beside those of the native gods that they most closely resembled. Even Indian fugitives brought the brother-gods, Demetr and Gisanes, whose images were not like those of the other gods of Armenia, for the images of the gods of Armenia are, as a rule, small, whereas these were very tall, with long black hair and black faces. There was also a great immigration of Jews into Armenia, and this influenced the Armenians in the direction of monotheism. Besides the principal gods, there were also secondary ones. These were spirits, corresponding to angels, who acted as guardians to different classes of natural objects: – *Kadjk* [which means "brave ones" in Armenian], who occupied the mountains; *Parik*, who presided over flocks; and many others.

Water was honoured in Armenia as a masculine principle. According to Tacitus (*Annals*, vi. 37) the Armenians offered horses as sacrifices to the Euphrates, and divined by its waves and foam. Sacred cities were built around the river Araxes and its tributaries. Even now there are many sacred springs with healing powers, and the people always feel a certain veneration towards waters in motion.

There were gods who lived in the waters and destroyed

harmful monsters of the deep. There was also a god who breathed out a mysterious atmosphere which destroyed malignant creatures. ... All the gods of this class were friendly to agriculturists.

There were also "*Haurot-Maurot*," the name of a flower (*Hyacinthus racemosus dodonei*) first mentioned by Agathangelos. The Arabs incorporated them in the Quran (ii. 96) as two angels sent down to live in Babel in human circumstances.

Alk, who dwelt in the waters, was a very harmful devil. He used to live in the corners of houses and stables, and in damp places. He had eyes of fire, nails of copper, teeth of iron, and the jaws of a wild boar. He carried a sword of iron in his hand and was a bitter enemy to pregnant women, near whom he sat at the time their child was born.

There were nymphs, who were guardians of women. They wandered through gardens and amid streams, but were invisible. They attended weddings and frequented bathrooms and the women's quarters in general. These nymphs and spirits were innumerable. Every woman was supposed to have a guardian nymph. The nymphs were supposed by some to be immortal and endowed with perpetual youth; others described them as mortal though they never grew old. There was also a group of male spirits who were regarded by some as mortal, by others as immortal. They wandered with the nymphs through forests, gardens, and other open places. They were imagined as very tall, with features like those of men; some were half-man and half-animal. Some were called *Parik*, "dancers"; others *Hushka parik*, "dancers to a melody in a minor key."

In some places, even now, a belief in these nymphs (or fairies) survives. Many stories are told of their beauty, their marvellous dancing, and their wondrous music. They are never called by the name of "nymphs," but are spoken of by the people of the country as "our betters." Still in some parts of Armenia, in May and October, a festival is held annually in honour of them, generally by the women in the Public Baths. They assemble early in the morning and remain till late at night, dancing, eating, and bathing. Before the people thought of building temples, they worshipped their gods in forests and on mountains. One of these forests was the Forest of Sos. According to tradition, the son of Ara the Beautiful, Anushavan, who devoted himself to the worship of this sacred place, was called, after the forest, Sos. The priests derived oracles from the rustling of the leaves in this holy wood.

Besides temples, which were numerous in Armenia, there were, all over the country, altars and shrines, as well as images and pictures.

To sum up, the pre-Christian religion of Armenia was at first a kind of nature-worship, which developed into polytheism (Boyajian, 1916, pp.127-131).A great many curious ceremonies are observed by the Armenians in connection with such family events as births, marriages, and deaths. A wedding takes a whole week to celebrate, and when a wealthy farmer dies all the inhabitants of the village are publicly invited by the priest in church to the funeral feast. They have also retained a great many strange superstitious practices, and believe in the existence of a variety of supernatural beings possessing propensities and powers both benevolent and malevolent. In the long winter nights, when the snow lies thick in the streets and on the housetops, the women fancy they hear in the howling of the wind the shouts and laughter of these tricksy beings. And the young women and girls, when the day's tasks are done, gather round the grandmother, who relates strange creepy stories of the pranks of the djinns, or charming romances dealing with peris, magicians and enchanted palaces, while the grandfather, sitting cross-legged in his fur-lined pelisse in the corner of the divan, tells the boys tales of the Armenian heroes of old (Lucy Garnett, *Turkish Life in Town and Country*, London, 1904, pp.176-82).

The Girl who changed into a Boy

There was and there wasn't, once upon a time there was an old woman who had one daughter. Since she was an only child, the old woman dressed her daughter in boys' clothes, so that she could play with the neighbours' children.

Now one day the King's daughter got lost, and was found by the old woman's daughter, who took her to her mother, and said:

'I have found this little child. Let us keep her.'

So the old woman kept the girl.

The King ordered a proclamation to be made throughout the land, announcing:

'My daughter is lost. Whosoever shall find her may request of me what he will.'

This announcement came to the old woman's ears, and she informed the King that it must be his daughter who was living with her. One of the King's ministers mounted a fine mare called Lulizar (Persian, 'Pearly-face') and came to the old woman's house to fetch the princess. The old woman's daughter went back with them, and on the way, Lulizar whispered to her:

'When the King asks you to make a wish, tell him you desire to possess me, and nothing else.'

When they came into the presence of the King, he embraced his daughter, and turning to the old woman's child, said:

'Make a wish, and I shall grant it.'

'Long life to Your Majesty,' said she. 'I should like to possess Lulizar.'

'Lulizar is worth my entire kingdom,' said the King. 'If I give her to you, I might as well give you my daughter too!'

And so he did.

The wedding feast lasted for seven days and for seven nights. It was not long before the princess realized that her husband was a woman like herself, and she ran to her mother, the Queen.

'A curse on you and your kingdom,' she cried, 'for marrying your daughter to a woman! He is a woman, as I am a woman! What shall I do?'

The Queen told the King.

'What shall we do?' said His Majesty. 'If we chop off his-her!-head, it will not help much, and if we do not, our daughter will be very miserable. There is nothing for it. Let us send him to some place from whence he will never return.'

He called his 'son-in-law'.

'My boy,' he said, 'you must go and fetch me the brother of Lulizar.'

The 'husband' got up, went to the stables to find Lulizar, and burst into tears.

'Why are you weeping, girl?' said the mare.

'The King has commanded me to find your brother and fetch him back here!' she lamented. 'How can I do that?'

'Ask the King for a bottle of old wine and a bundle of wool,' said Lulizar. 'Then we shall leave together to find my brother.'

The girl followed his instructions, then led Lulizar from the stables, mounted, and rode off.

Eventually, they came to the sea. Not far from the shore stood a marble fountain.

'Go over to that fountain,' said the horse. 'Empty the basin, block up the spout with the bundle of wool, and fill the basin with wine in place of the water. Then conceal yourself. My brother will emerge from the sea, gulp down the wine, and grow dizzy. Then you must run forward and leap on to his back. He will gallop towards the sea, but you must shout, "Whoah! Your sister calls you!", and he will turn round and come over to me.'

The girl did as Lulizar told her. The sea-horse came out of the waves, sniffed the air, and drank the wine. When it grew dizzy, the girl emerged from her hiding place and jumped on its back. The stallion galloped furiously towards the sea, but the girl shouted, 'Whoah! Whoah! Your sister calls you!' Lulizar bounded up, her brother joined her, and they all returned to the palace, where the girl gave Lulizar's brother to the King.

When the princess saw that her 'husband' had come back, she blazed with anger.

'May you and your kingdom perish!' she cried. 'Rid me of that woman!'

The King summoned his chamberlain.

'He-she!-has come back,' he said. 'What must we do to get rid of him-her!-for ever?'

'Send her to the House of Devs, Sire,' said the chamberlain. 'Let her try to collect the seven years' arrears of taxes they owe us. She will stand no chance of escaping from them!'

The King summoned his 'son-in-law'.

'My boy,' he said, 'the devs owe us for seven years' taxes. Go and collect it for me.'

The girl got up and went to find Lulizar in the stables and burst into tears.

'Lulizar,' she wept. 'I am in your hands as you are in God's. The King has asked me to go to the House of the Devs and collect the taxes for the past seven years.'

'Do not cry,' said Lulizar. 'We shall collect them, never fear!'

The girl mounted her horse and they rode away. Eventually they came to the huge white marble gates of the House of the Devs. The gates were tightly shut.

'Tie my tail to the marble gates,' said the horse. 'I shall pull them open, and then you may go in and fetch the taxes.'

The girl tied the mare's tail to the marble gates, Lulizar pulled and tugged, and the dust flew up in clouds. Finally the gates burst open, and the girl slipped in. She suddenly found herself face to face with forty devs.

'Aha!' they chuckled. 'Our dinner has just walked in!'

'I don't know how you can sit there like that,' said the girl, 'when the King is about to confiscate all the marble in your quarry as compensation for your seven years' arrears of taxes!'

The devils rushed out to inspect their quarry. The girl looked rapidly around her, saw the seven years' arrears in a money bag hanging on a pillar, and had snatched it down, untied Lulizar, jumped on her back, and galloped away before the devs had time to collect their wits. Horse and rider returned to the palace, where the girl handed the King the seven years' arrears of taxes.

When the princess saw that her 'husband' was back again, she was furious, and ran to her father at once.

'Why do you not destroy that woman?' she demanded angrily.

The King once again summoned his chamberlain.

'She has escaped from the House of the Devs!' he said. 'What must we do to get rid of her for ever?'

'Sire,' said the chamberlain, 'your grandfather once had a valuable rosary which the devs stole and presented to their mother. Send her to get it back. She will never be able to escape from that old she-devil!'

The King summoned his 'son-in-law'.

'My boy,' he said, 'go and bring back my grandfather's rosary, which is now in the hands of the mother of the devs.'

The girl got up, went to find Lulizar in the stables, and burst into tears.

'Why are you weeping, girl?' asked Lulizar.

'The King has commanded me to fetch his grandfather's rosary, which is now in the hands of the mother of the devs,' she sobbed. 'How can I do that?'

'Do not worry, girl,' said the mare. 'God is great. We shall fetch the rosary'.

The girl mounted Lulizar, and they rode away, until at last they came to the castle which was the home of the mother of the devs.

The castle was built on a high mountain peak overlooking a deep ravine.

'When you enter the mother devil's castle,' said Lulizar, 'you will find her sleeping with her back propped up against a column. The rosary hangs on that very same column. At the first stroke of every hour, the rosary drops into her hands, and she begins to count her beads. When you see it begin to fall, snatch it away before it touches her hands, rush out with it, and leap straight out into the ravine. I shall be waiting on the road below, and shall catch you on my back.'

The girl went up to the castle, passed through the main gate, found the mother of the devs asleep against the column as Lulizar had said, and hid behind it. The hour struck, and the rosary started to fall into the she-devil's hand. The girl darted forward, seized the rosary as it fell, rushed out of the castle, and leapt straight off the edge of the wall into the ravine. Lulizar rose half-way up in the air, and caught her in her saddle. Awakened by the noise, the mother of the devs started up. She saw in a flash that her rosary had gone, and that she had no chance of catching the rider now galloping furiously away on a horse that moved like the wind.

She racked her brains in search of her most terrible curse. She found it.

'My curse upon thee!' she shrieked. 'If thou be a man, be now woman! If thou be woman, be now man!'

In the twinkling of an eye the young girl turned into a young man.

Lulizar and her rider returned to the palace, where the young man gave the King his grandfather's long-lost rosary, and then went to greet his princess.

This time when the princess came to see her father, she was not angry.

'I find that my husband is a man after all,' she said. 'I would not change him for any other, so I beg you to stop sending him on perilous missions!'

The King gave the young couple a wealthy city to govern for

themselves, and they all ate, drank, and made merry, and lived happy ever after.

Three apples dropped from Heaven: one for the story-teller, one for him who listens, and one for him who marks it well. (*Tgha dardzogh akhchikë,* told in 1913 by the illiterate watermill-keeper Avetis Nazarian of Oshakan village, province of Ayrarat; translated from the version reproduced in I. Orbeli and S. Taronian, *Hay zhogovrdakan heqiathner* [Armenian Popular Tales], a series of volumes published in Yerevan between 1959 and 1967, and published in Downing, C. (1972) *Armenian Folk-Tales and Fables,* Oxford: Oxford University Press.)

***

Animals as supernatural helpers feature prominently in Armenian folktales, and their function is to dispense both magic and advice. And from the moment Lulizar the mare whispers to the old woman's daughter on the way back to the palace of the King, the story becomes an account of a journey, and a journey on which the "rules" of ordinary reality no longer apply. Not only does Lulizar function as a supernatural or spirit helper, but she also speaks with a human voice. So either the story is set in a time when humans and animals spoke the same language or the fact that the old woman's daughter and the mare are able to communicate with each other is indicative that this is a shamanic encounter and that the journey is a shamanic one.

Many events in stories are set in or on vehicles of transportation, such as the ship in *The Book of Jonah* for example, and the setting serves the purpose of temporarily suspending "the safe predictability and clarity of the social order" (Bal, 2004, p.217). In this particular story it is Lulizar who is the vehicle.

As for the importance of the horse, it is worth noting what Eliade has to say on the association between the animal and the shaman's drum, and the way in which the drum has traditionally been used in a number of cultures by shamans to induce the trancelike state required for journeying:

> The iconography of the drums is dominated by the symbolism of the ecstatic journey, that is, by journeys that imply a break-through in plane and hence a "Center of the World." The drumming at the beginning of the séance, intended to summon the spirits and "shut them up" in the shaman's drum, constitutes the preliminaries for the ecstatic journey. This is why the drum is called the "shaman's horse" (Yakut, Buryat). The Altaic drum bears a representation of a horse; when the shaman drums, he is believed to go to the sky on his horse. Among the Buryat, too, the drum made with a horse's hide represents that animal (Eliade, 1989, p.173).

According to Yakut beliefs, the horse is of divine origin. In the beginning God is said to have created a horse from which a half-horse, half-man descended, and from this being humankind was born. The Sky-Horse deity, Uordakh-Djesegei, plays a major role in Yakut religion, and Yakut mythology depicts many other scenes in which deities and guardian spirits descend to the earth as horses. The honorable goddess Ajjyst, the patron of childbearing, appears as a white mare, as does the goddess called Lajahsit. The horse is of great significance to the shaman too. "A Yakut shaman's healing performance is unthinkable without a horse, just as the entire ceremony cannot occur without the shaman's participation … A horse, its image, or at times, an object personifying the animal is always present in the shaman's preparations and performances" (Diachenko, 1994, p.266).

As for the reference by Eliade to the horse being known as the Yakut shaman's drum, it is actually the coat the Yakut shaman wears that is believed to give him the supernatural power needed to go to other worlds, and it is this that is called the 'shaman's horse' (see Czaplicka, 2007, p.67).

Among Turkic-speaking people of South Siberia, including Tuvinians, the horse can play an important role too, and it is the drum that can represent the animal ridden by shamans to travel to other worlds. Its handle can be regarded as the horse's "spine; the plaits of leather attached to the upper part of the ring symbolize the reins of the horse; the drumstick is a lash, which beats a drum only in certain places" (Diakonova, 1994, p.253).

> Whether he is chosen by gods or spirits to be their mouthpiece, or is predisposed to this function by physical defects, or has a heredity that is equivalent to a magico-religious vocation, the medicine man stands apart from the world of the profane precisely because he has more direct relations with the sacred and manipulates its manifestations more effectively. Infirmity, nervous disorder, spontaneous vocation, or heredity are so many external signs of a "choice," an "election." Sometimes these signs are physical (an innate or acquired infirmity); sometimes an accident, even of the commonest type, is involved (e.g., falling from a tree or being bitten by a snake); ordinarily … election is announced by an unusual accident or event – lightning, apparition, dream, and so on (Eliade, 1989, pp.31.32).

Let us now move on to consider the cross-dressing that features in the tale. In southern Borneo, the Ngadju-Dayak have a special category of hermaphrodite-shamans known as *basir*, which translates as "unable to reproduce". However, whether they are truly hermaphrodites, or men who dress as women, remains unclear. Another example can be found among the Chukchee - the spirit guides of male shamans oblige them to dress as women and they sometimes even take husbands. According to Bogoras, the same category of shaman was also found among the Koryak, the Kamchadul, and the Asiatic Eskimo and he refers to them as "persons of a changed sex" (Bogoras, 1909, p.456).

Bogoras even provides us with a description:

> Tilu'wgi's face, encircled with braids of thick hair arranged after the manner of Chukchee women, looked very different from masculine faces. It was something like a female tragic mask fitted to the body of a giantess of a race different from our own. All the ways of this strange creature were decidedly feminine. He was so 'bashful,' that whenever I asked a question of somewhat indiscreet character, you could see, under the layer of its usual dirt, a blush spread over his face, and he would cover his eyes with his sleeve, like a young beauty of sixteen. I heard him gossip with the female neighbors in a most feminine way, and even saw him hug small children with evident envy for the joys of motherhood (Bogoras, 1909, pp.453-454).

Borgoras also gives an example of a female to male gender transformation of a shaman and how delicate matters of sex were taken care of – by means of a "gastrocnemius from the leg of a reindeer, fastened to a broad leather belt" (Bogoras, 1909, pp.455-56). In the Caucasus however, apart from what we find in this particular tale, there are no such recorded examples of female to male gender transformations.

The occasional androgyny of the shaman can be regarded as one inflection of paradise, where the two become one. As Joan Halifax observes, the dissolution of opposites, such as life and death or male and female, and the subsequent "making whole again" is one of the main features in the initiation and transformation process as experienced by the shaman, at least in the case of indigenous forms of shamanism (see Ripinsky-Naxon, 1993, pp.84-85). Looking at the same phenomena from another angle, the way we have been conditioned to see everything in terms of binary logic, makes it hard to apprehend more analogical and ternary belief-systems despite all the exceptions to the supposed rule (see Dumont, 1983).

The early recorders of shamanic practices no doubt considered themselves to be enlightened by the standards of the times in which they were living. Fashions and standards change though, and today they would be considered by many to be nothing more than racist and sexist imperialists. The following quote, on the subject of transvestism among male Chukchee shamans who dressed and lived as women, serves to exemplify the point: 'The perversion of the sexual functions, resulting from psychical or physical causes, may happen among primitive peoples as well as among civilized ones' (Bogoras, 1909, p.455). The way in which the shamanic practices were recorded was clearly colored by the prejudices of the "outsiders" who did the job. Today we are often witness to the other extreme, "insiders" who go native and do everything they can to paint an idyllic picture of the world they inhabit temporarily and its people – who they live with and grow attached to. As a result, in the case of both the "outsiders" and the "insiders", the material collected by them has to be subject to a great deal of critical scrutiny before any meaningful conclusions can be drawn from it.

As for cross-dressing in the Caucasus, the manuscripts of the Hippocratic authors portray the mysterious Enareis or Anaries, who are also incidentally mentioned by Herodotus,

> as a category of Scythian men who have become – in their social behaviour – women. 'The great majority among the Scythians become impotent, do women's work, live like women and converse accordingly.' These men are explicitly described as cross-dressers: they 'put on women's clothes, holding that they have lost their manhood'. They take this step after finding that they are unable to have sexual intercourse, thinking that 'they have sinned against Heaven' (Ascherson, 2007, p.121).

Representations of magical androgynous figures can also be found on Scythian, Sarmatian and Indo-Iranian decorations.

According to the deconstructionists, polarities and privileged positions are simply arbitrary human constructions, and "objective reality" does not exist (see Hansen, 2001, p. 64). Shamans can be regarded as master deconstructionalists. By consorting with spirits, they regularly deconstruct the polarity of life and death, and by their adoption of an alternative lifestyle the Chuchkee shamans can be seen to be doing just the same. One can even argue it is essential for shamans to deconstruct order, especially if a person's or a community's rigidity of outlook have blocked adaptation and growth, and they need to view their situation in a new light in order to remove the impasse.

In this particular tale though, the gender confusion can perhaps best be accounted for in a different way. It can be regarded as being representative of the initiatory sickness that traditionally befalls those who receive the shamanic "call" and is only resolved once the prospective candidate stops fighting against the process and accepts his or her fate. Thus the gender resolution can be seen as the restoration of balance to the community, which traditionally was the shaman's main concern.

Also worthy of note is the fact that "The wedding feast lasted for seven days and for seven nights", with seven surely not being an arbitrary number plucked out of the blue, but being included in the tale for a reason.

> Seven is a mystic or sacred number in many different traditions. Among the Babylonians and Egyptians, there were believed to be seven planets, and the alchemists recognized seven planets too. In the Old Testament there are seven days in creation, and for the Hebrews every seventh year was Sabbatical too. There are seven virtues, seven sins, seven ages in the life of man, seven wonders of the world, and the number seven repeatedly occurs in the *Apocalypse* as well. The Muslims talk of there being seven heavens, with the seventh being formed of divine light that is beyond the power of words to describe, and the Kabbalists also believe there are seven heavens –each arising above the other, with the seventh being the abode of God (Berman, 2008a, p.122).

Moreover, this is by no means the only reference to the number seven that can be found in Armenian folklore. In the Yazidi belief system, the world is now in the care of a *Heptad* of seven Holy Beings, known as angels or *heft sirr* (the Seven Mysteries). Additionally, the number also features in an Armenian spring festival that was held until recent times. Young women, in great secrecy, would go up onto the mountain to cut Haurot and Maurot flowers (species of hyacinth). "In the meantime, others, who were hiding from the first group, drew water from seven springs or rivers. In the evening, the flowers and the water were poured together into a basin called Hagvir. The liquor which resulted was a potion for happiness" (Bonnefoy, 1993, p.266).

Although the cosmology described in Creation Myths will vary from culture to culture, the structure of the whole cosmos is in fact frequently symbolized by the number seven, made up of the four directions, the centre, the zenith in heaven, and the nadir in the underworld. In other words, the essential axes of this structure are the four cardinal points and a central vertical axis passing through their point of intersection that connects the Upper World, the Middle World and the Lower World. As for the names by which the central vertical axis that connects the three worlds is referred to, these include the world pole, the tree of life, the sacred mountain, the central house pole, and Jacob's ladder.

It has been proposed that "Every wonder tale is rich in the use of magic and must have some task for its hero to accomplish ... various physical qualities enable the hero to overcome great obstacles. Frequently, he is aided by superhuman companions in fulfilling tasks. These helpers have great prowess in running, throwing, eating, hearing, drinking and lifting" (Hoogasian-Villa, 1966, p.69). In *The Girl who changed into a Boy* the hero/heroine is set three such tasks to accomplish – to fetch the brother of Lulizar, to collect seven years' arrears of taxes from the House of the Devs, and to bring back the valuable rosary that belonged to the King's grandfather from the mother of the Devs – and Lulizar is the supernatural companion. There is a problem, however, with the term "wonder tale" as it fails to fully acknowledge the probable origin of the kind of story we are considering here, the way in which it more than likely dates back to pre-Christian times (despite the mention of the rosary, which is probably a later addition). And it is for this reason the term "shamanic story" is to be preferred.

The shamanic journey frequently involves passing through some kind of gateway. As Eliade explains,

> The "clashing of rocks," the "dancing reeds," the gates in the shape of jaws, the "two razor-edged restless mountains," the "two clashing icebergs," the "active door," the "revolving barrier," the door made of the two halves of the eagle's beak, and many more – all these are images used in myths and sagas to suggest the insurmountable difficulties of passage to the Other World [and sometimes the passage back too] (Eliade, 2003, pp.64-65).

In *The Girl who changed into a Boy* the huge white marble gates of the House of the Devs and the inaccessible castle built on a high mountain peak overlooking a deep ravine present just such difficulties for the hero/heroine of the tale. It is also frequently the case that to make such a journey requires a change in one's mode of being, entering a transcendent state, which makes it possible to attain the world of spirit. Sometimes when we are faced with overwhelming difficulties, we find an inner strength we never knew we had, and perhaps this helps to explain how our heroine attains the necessary state that enables her to achieve her goal.

It has been suggested that the purpose of the descent, "as universally exemplified in the myth of the hero is to show that only in the region of danger ... can one find the 'treasure hard to attain' " (Jung, 1968, pp.335-336) and this is borne out by what transpires in the tale. For although our hero is unable to see Lulizar waiting at the base of the castle walls, far below her, she is required to leap "straight off the edge of the wall into the ravine" in order to achieve her goal, in the same way that Carlos Castaneda had to make such a leap of faith into the abyss at the end of his semi-autobiographical novel *Tales of Power* (1974). What we can see from this is that for shamanic work to be effective, being able to trust in the process is imperative.

It can be argued that perhaps the defining characteristic and main attribute of the shaman has traditionally been his or her mastery of the ability to journey at will to other realities to intercede with the spirits on behalf of clients and to bring back information to help them with their dilemmas, thus working to restore balance to the community. What we find by the end of the tale is that the old woman's daughter has had her own balance restored as a result of her initiatory journey, and will thus be better able to help others with their problems in future. In other words, she has become a "wounded healer".

The person traditionally chosen to be the shaman of a community was often a wounded healer – someone who had been through a near-death experience and who was consequently well-suited to helping others through difficult times in their lives. The experience would establish the healer's warrant to minister to his people's needs as one who knew how to control disorder. The profession to which the concept of the wounded healer most aptly applies today is probably that of the psychoanalyst and the kind of shamanism that has been practised by tribal peoples through the ages can thus be viewed as a form of pre-scientific psychotherapy (see Lewis, 2003, p.172).

So what we find is that *The Girl who changed into a Boy* includes all the elements one would expect it to do as a typical example of its genre – a heroine who does not really fit in (in this case to due to her/his gender ambiguity), a heroine who is able to understand the language of the animals and communicate with them, a spirit helper in the form of the mare Lulizar, a journey into non-ordinary reality that entails facing barriers that have to be crossed and quests that have to be accomplished, "shape-shifting" (of the heroine from woman into man), and finally the restoration of the equilibrium of the community. This is brought about as a result of the gender transformation of the old woman's daughter and then the presumably successful consummation of the marriage between the two young people. All this indicates that what we have here is essentially a shamanic story rather than what at first sight might appear to be just a simple fairy tale, and the same will be shown to be the case with the other stories included in this study.

Chapter 3

Chechnya & Ingushetia

The Chechens live in a small territory called Chechnya bordered by Daghestan to the east and northeast; Ingushetia and North Ossetia to the west; Russia's Stravrapol Province and Cossack region to the north; and Georgia to the south and southwest. The Caucasus Mountains, which stretch along a line 1,100 kilometres long between the Black Sea and Caspian Sea, protect the people not only from enemies but from outside influences in general. The Chechens therefore have retained many traditional customs and practices. Not only has the mountainous terrain long been strategically important for Chechnya, but it also supports sheep farming – the traditional Chechen occupation. As for the size of the population, according to the 2002 Russian census there were 1,088,816 people living in Chechnya, but that does not include the tens of thousands of refugees who, as a result of the recent conflicts, are now living in the neighboring regions.

It is said that

> when God created the world, he sprinkled nations over the globe, but clumsily dropped his shaker over what ancient travellers called the "mountain of languages". Pliny wrote that the ancient Greeks needed 300 interpreters to conduct business in the North Caucasus, while later, "we Romans conducted our affairs there with the aid of 130 interpreters." Today the mountains remain a living language laboratory. In Dagestan, one village may speak Avar, the next village Darghin, the next Lezghin. There are three main linguistic groups: Turkic, such as Karachai and Balkar; Indo-European, such as Ossetian, which is related to Persian; and the truly indigenous Caucasian tongues.

> The Caucasian languages, which are not found anywhere else in the world, are themselves divided into two branches: the eastern, such as Chechen, Ingush, and several Dagestani languages, and the western Adygei dialects, spoken by the Adygei, Cherkess, Kabards and Abkhaz (Smith, 2006, pp.7-8).

Contrary to popular misconception, the Chechens are not Slavs and they are not Turkic in origin either, despite the fact that Turkey unites all North Caucasus Muslims into a category which is related to them. In fact, they are not even "Chechen" as this was a term coined by the Russians after the name of a village (Chechen-aul) where the Russians first encountered the people in the early 16th century. The first written mention of the inhabitants of the region was in the 7th century, when they were known as the "Nokhchii" (pronounced "No-h-chee" with the "h" pronounced as when gargling from the back of the mouth: very similar to one of the ancient Aramaic letters). Ethnically, they are related to other groups throughout the Caucasus, most closely with the neighboring Ingush. Together, the Nokhchii and Ingush people have been called the "Vainaikh" which means "Our People." They have lived where they are now since prehistoric times, and while the Mesopotamians, Persians, Turks, Mongols, Slavs and others have greatly influenced the region with their wars, conquests and trade, being fiercely proud and protective of their roots and background, the inhabitants of Chechnya have remained ethnically the same for thousands of years.

As for the Nokhchii language, it is considered to be both one of the most difficult and oldest languages in the Caucasus. Its roots can be traced most closely to the ancient Mesopotamians. A cuneiform-style of writing is evident on some of the stone inscriptions, dating at least to 2,800 BC. The Nokhchii language, as we know it today, is most linked to some of the words used by the ancient Akkhadians, and can be traced at least to 1200 BC. It is not related to Russian, Slavic, Indo-European or Turkish languages.

But linguistic influences from invaders and traders over the centuries, including Mongolian and Arabic, are evident in many words. Linguistically, the Nokhchii language belongs to the Nakh branch of Caucasian languages, which include Ingush (galgai) and Batsbi (found in present-day Georgia). Until Islamic tradition came in and words were transcribed phonetically into Arabic it was purely an oral language. In the early 19th century the Russians changed it to Latin, and then the Soviets in the 20th century changed it to Cyrillic. However, it is now written in Latin again.

The history of the Nokhchii, and their land, is filled with rich and colorful stories, which have survived for thousands of years through oral traditions that have been passed down generation by generation through clan elders. However, legends have blended with actual events so that the true history is difficult to write. During the 19th century, several Chechen writers tried to preserve the history in massive volumes. Some still survive, despite Stalin's purges between 1939-1944, which ended with the exile of all Chechen and Ingush peoples as well as the removal of all references to the Chechen people from maps, history books and more. The 1994-1996 war destroyed most of Chechnya's treasured archaeological and historical sites, though fortunately ancient burial sites, architectural monuments and several prehistoric cave petroglyphs still remain in the mountains. These valuable relics, coupled with the histories and stories of the elders, provide the people with virtually the only remaining evidence of who their ancient ancestors were.

Despite the fact that the people are predominantly Sunni Muslim today, that was not always so. Before the adoption of Islam, the Nokhchii people practised their own blend of religious traditions and beliefs. Like so many ancient cultures and civilizations worldwide, archaeological evidence and modern-day practices suggest that their ancient religion was based on cycles of nature and astronomy, with many gods and complex rituals. Artefacts and monuments, as well as burial and sacrificial sites, tell archaeologists a lot about the religious beliefs before Islam and Christianity. Petroglyphs in underground caverns high in the mountains, dating from at least 4,000 BC, depict solar signs, anthropomorphic animals, and use of plants for rituals. Ancient underground burial vaults from approximately 2,600 BC have carved niches and unusual stones with concentric circles in a variety of manners. Different underground dwellings dating from 1,200 BC until the 9th or 10th centuries AD suggest a wide variety of gods associated with forces of nature and the stars. Islam was slowly introduced over a period of centuries, gaining converts by the 15th & 16th centuries, but not taking root until well into the 18th to mid-19th centuries, with the mountain regions last.

Then, after the tsarist era, instead of the freedom they had been led to believe would be theirs, the people got Communist atheism, Russian language, Russian officials and brutal land collectivization. Mosques were either shut down or destroyed, and the mullahs arrested or shot. However, new mosques sprang up under Soviet President Mikhail Gorbachev's *glasnost* thaw in 1987, and by the 1990s could be seen everywhere. Along with the mosques came Islamic schools, or *medressehs*, a renewal of Arabic studies, and even pilgrimages to Mecca. However, "Many people across the region were so ignorant about Islam that this was often less a revival than a rediscovery. The middle-aged had grown up in an atheist state, while their children were just as likely to be inspired by the thought of making money and becoming post-Soviet consumers as they were by the mosque" (Smith, 2006, p.75). So what we find today in Chechnya are ancient traditions and superstitions blended with traditional Islamic beliefs and practices, and post-Soviet consumerism. It is a unique mixture and unlike any other.

What the majority of the people actually practise is a localized Sufi tradition and, as a result and contrary to popular misconception, the puritanical Islamicists in practice have almost no support from Chechen society in general. The fact that they follow the Sufi *tariqat*, or religious path, has stood them in good stead in that it has proved to be

> the ideal form of religion for facing outside cultural and military pressure. Sufism has no need for formal buildings such as mosques, and its undocumented but fanatically loyal members can easily go underground or surface whenever they choose. ... The *zikr* ritual formed an unbreakable shield around these people's sense of identity and self-confidence. The tightly knit groups which gathered everywhere, and still gather, to perform the *zikr* were perfectly equipped for battle. Many were unafraid to die, because they felt close to Allah, and their training in brotherhood had prepared them to act as a group, with the discipline vital to fighting (Smith, 2006, p.40).

A further illustration of the importance of the *zikr* to the people can be seen from how,

> When Jokhar Dudayev seized power in 1991, the *zikr* became a political spectacle, and dozens of dancers gathered in the central square in Grozny and danced more and more furiously. When the Russians were poised to invade, it became an independence dance as one desperate dancer ran around the circle brandishing a Chechen flag, pressed in by a crowd of rhythmically clapping people (Gall & de Waal, 1997, pp.32-33).

As for the practice of shamanism in Chechnya, we know that at least one of the roles traditionally performed by a shaman – that of acting as intermediary between the people and the gods or spirits – was performed by the priests of the Vainakh:

> Men of cloth were wrapped up in halos of sanctity and were clad in white. A priest (*ts'uu*) was the first to address the deity in prayer and he alone could enter the sanctuary at will. He was

the one to go for counsel in lean years or in case of illness.

We know too that the Vainakh priests acted as diviners and interpreted dreams, again roles traditionally performed by shamans:

> They also acted as medicine men and sorcerers, auguring, among other things, the harvest and weather. Like their Pharaonic counterparts, Vainakh priests had recourse to oneirocriticism, or interpretation of dreams, to divine the wishes of the gods. For example, the spirits inspired dreamers as to the sites where shrines were to be built (Jaimoukha, 2005, p.115).

Additionally, the shaman of a community was often called on to arbitrate to settle disputes, another role undertaken by the Vainakh priests:

> Vainakh priests were responsible for maintaining social stability and settling civil law issues. They did not cultivate the land for sustenance, relying on villagers to till the fields assigned to them instead. The clergy were presented with offerings from their parishes, including jewellery, as can be attested by the discovery of gems in temples (Jaimoukha, 2005, p.115).

So it would seem that all the most important functions of the shaman were fulfilled by the Vainakh priests, though whether they actually entered trance states in the course of their work remains unclear. However, given the popularity of the mystic dance among followers of the Sufi *tariqat* or religious path, it would seem that people in the region have a natural propensity for doing so, which would suggest that even though we lack concrete evidence, it was very likely to have been the case.

Historically, the people's lives revolve around their village and clan structures, and this has been the case since ancient times. Taips, or clans, consist of several villages with a common ancestor, and each village can have anywhere from 10-50 families. There are more than 125 clans among the Nokhchii people, and all are categorized by a specific "tukum", which is like a tribe. There are 9 tukums and legend has it that they all share a common family ancestry of 9 brothers, hence the 9 stars on the Chechen flag. Members of the 9 tukums unite to help one another, just as the legendary 9 brothers did thousands of years ago.

While the clans share a common history, language, religion and culture, each taip has their own elder council, court of justice, cemetery, customs, traditions and adats (which were customary laws). Leadership is by election and each clan, or taip, is self-sufficient and self-contained. The unity of clans, despite blood feuds, has traditionally been strong, and it remains strongest in the mountain regions. The clan structure has protected the people for thousands of years, and is one of the main reasons why foreign invaders, and later Russia, could not penetrate the country and conquer the people. As elders ruled in ancient days, today they are the backbone of village and clan life, and have the respect of all the people. Not only do the Chechen elders often act as intermediaries between feuding families but they also acted as intermediaries between villages and besieging Russian troops during the recent war, sometimes even deciding whether their village would fight or not (see Smith, 2006, p.23). Consequently, even though an elected government now exists, it is still the elders and the taips that truly rule. And the 9 tukums unite them all.

Taip membership ties a Chechen to what is, in effect, a large extended family, whose members provide support for the weak and work for the unemployed.

> A more recent development is that they should help each other to do deals in the black economy. There is a strong parallel with Sicily's ties of honour and blood, which gave birth to the Mafia and are much firmer than any obligations to the state (Gall & de Waal, 1997, p.26).

Hospitality and respect for guests was, and still is, a source of pride for all Caucasian peoples, and the Chechens are no exception.

> In classical Chechen society, a cult had developed around hospitality, bestowing reverence upon the guest (*haasha*; cf. Circassian *hesch'e*). Turpal Nokhcho (literally: "Hero-Chechen"), the legendary ancestor of the Chechens, was born with a piece of iron in one hand and a portion of cheese in the other. Many legends and sayings have come down to us depicting the high status and some details of this institution. The inhospitable terrain and inclement weather had a lot to do with the development of this institution. Hospitality was certainly an important and interesting aspect of the social life of the Vainakh.
>
> Chechens received their guests with open arms, literally, as a token of sincerity and absence of malice. The etiquette of proper guest reception, lodging and subsequent delivery to the next destination or host (*heeshan daa*) was very involved. All Chechens were conversant with proper table manners and seating arrangements at home and as guests. A guest was not only put up for as long as he wished, but was also lodged in the best quarters and offered the choicest victuals, sometimes at the expense of the host's family. He was always seated in the place of honour (*barch*) in a room or at the table. It was improper to enquire of the guest about the purpose of his visit in the first three days. Hospitality was not conditional and no compensation was expected, any offer in this regard being considered a grave insult. A guest, however, could present the children of his host with gifts.
>
> Refusing to receive a visitor, even if a fugitive or inveterate criminal, was a stigma that stuck for life. The guest in return was expected to follow specific rules of etiquette and not to overburden his host. He was also expected to lodge with the same host on his next visit to the village, failure to do so being

considered an indictable breach of etiquette (Jaimoukha, 2005, p.135).

When Chechens meet, they greet each other with the words "Marsha woghiyla" (masculine form), and "Marsha yoghiyla" (feminine form). This can be translated as: "When you come to this house or meeting place, freedom, peace and kindness are extended to you, they are in fact guaranteed to you as a guest".

In a Chechen home, guests can expect to receive the best food and the most pleasant accommodation that the hosts can afford, and the importance attached to providing hospitality is reflected in Chechen proverbs: "Beauty lasts till sunset, kindness lasts as long as you live", and "Serve a good meal to a bad guest but offer what you've got to a good man". However, the younger generation today tends to have a much more casual and relaxed attitude towards the treatment of guests, which tends to irritate the older generation. Visiting remains an important part of Chechen social life though, and guests are still expected to return invitations and extend hospitality to those who have entertained them in the past.

***

Very little is known about the early history of the Chechen people. Their background is unclear and surrounded by legends rather than historical documents. Moreover, attempting to uncover the ancient native culture is no easy matter for two further reasons, the first being the influence of the Avar imams. As leaders of the struggle of the Northeast Caucasians against Russian encroachment, they saw it as their duty to suppress the native culture in favor of spreading the Sufi ethos. The other reason is due to the conduct towards the Chechens by the Russians over the last three centuries, and what has been described as their "incessant drive to impose an adventitious set of morals and modes of conduct" on the people through "expulsion, transfer, mass deportations, massacres and full-scale invasions," all of which, not surprisingly, have "taken a very heavy toll on Chechen society" (see Jaimoukha, 2005, p.6).

> It has been suggested that the pre-Christian Vainakh had an amalgam of religions and cults, including animism, totemism, paganism, polytheism, familial-ancestral and agrarian and funereal cults. Stone sanctuaries and chapels were erected in honour of patrons in the mountain settlements. Objects of cultic rituals discovered at excavation sites include metallic amulets, hand-bells, deer-teeth, tips of arrows, ear-claws and human figurines. Subterranean petroglyphs, dating back to the fourth/fifth millennium BC, showed solar signs, figures of anthropomorphic animals, and plants (Jaimoukha, 2005, p.107).

However, was there in fact an amalgam of religions and cults, or were different religions and cults practised at different times and/or in different places? And why is there no mention of shamanism in this list? Possibly as it would not be recognized as a religion by the author, or perhaps due to the fact that he intended for it to be included under the heading of animism. Either way, we should certainly not take its omission as evidence of the fact that it was not practised or that it did not exist. In view of the themes to be found in the stories included in this volume, and what we know about what was being practised in neighbouring countries in pre-Christian times, this would surely be extremely unlikely. So let us assume then it was merely an oversight on the part of the author, and turn our attention instead to what the same author has to say about animism, probably the most ancient religion of the Vainakh (if one includes shamanism under this heading), and one that was prevalent among all peoples of the North Caucasus.

> Its origin probably dates back to the Palaeolithic Age, or the Old Stone Age, more than 10,000 years ago. ... The basic tenet of

> animism was the belief that a soul resided in every object, animate or inanimate, functioning as the motive force and guardian. In animistic thought, nature was all alive. In a future state the spirit would exist as part of an immaterial soul. The spirit, therefore, was thought to be universal. Ghosts, demons and deities inhabited almost all objects, rendering them subject to worship. Ritual services were associated with some of the more important sites, like (Mount) Ts'e-Lam and Lake Galanch'ozh. Khin-Naana (River-Motherland) was the guardian naiad of mountain rivers and Huenan-Naana (Forest-Mother) was the wood-nymph, or dryad (Jaimoukha, 2005, p.108).

What we also know from signs visible on extant ancient ruins is that

> the belief in magic and ghosts (*ghaalartash*) was widespread among the Vainakh. There were different forms of magic wielded by witches (*gheemash*), old sorceresses (*eeshapash* and *chabaabanash*) and warlocks. A special class of magicians, called "gham-sag" ('witch-human'), had the power to depart from their bodies and haunt those of animals [in other words, to shape-shift]. If during this spiritual transmigration the body was annihilated, the magician would have remained in limbo and eventually perished. Witches had special canes that could be turned into steeds when dyed with charm potions. In their defence against sorcery, mere mortals had recourse to amulets, the one made from quince (*haibanan dechig*) being also "effective" against injury and disease. Conjury (*bozbu-unchalla*) was practised by a special class of people called "bozbu-unchash" (Jaimoukha, 2005, p.151).

Additionally, we are informed that fortune-telling (*pal)* was a developed "craft", with there being

> special classes of people with vatic powers and a number of

> oracular devices, including a book of divinations (*zeeda-zhaina*: literally "star book"), at their disposal. Diviners would spend the night in a sanctuary, lying face down and keeping their ears pressed to the floor to hear the deity's revelations and convey them to an eager audience the next morning. Scapulimancers divined the future by scapulae, holding the ram shoulder-blades to the light and interpreting the marks, the spots predicting the harvest, weather and even familial events. In addition, women soothsayers sized pieces of cloth, wrapped spoons with cotton and used lithomancy, hyalomancy, akin to crystal-gazing, and catoptromancy to foretell the future. Auspices and augury had religious and practical applications, for example using the arrival of the hoopoe to predict the advent of spring (Jaimoukha, 2005, p.150).

It has to be said however that the picture we are presented with of this early period in Chechnya by Jaimoukha is really nothing more than a rough sketch and, as he admits himself,

> The animist-pagan period in Chechnya warrants more research to obtain a more comprehensive picture of the ancient cults and to establish connections with Near Eastern civilizations in antiquity. The pictograms and magic signs on stone towers and tombs would provide crucial clues, as they often date back to earlier periods than the structures themselves (Jaimoukha, 2005, p.109).

Although Chechnya's medieval architecture has not been sufficiently studied by architectural historians, the limited study that has been done already shows the existence of common elements between the material and artistic culture of Chechnya and the civilizations of Asia Minor and the Mediterranean. These connections will become better understood with more extensive research of ancient Chechen pagan religions and mythology, which demonstrate numerous parallels with the pagan gods and mythological heroes of the great civilizations of the ancient world. In that aspect, the pictograms and magical signs on the stone towers and tombs are very interesting to scholars, as they often date from an earlier period than the structures themselves. These towers and tombs were often built using stones taken from more ancient buildings, some of which dated from the 7th to the 5th centuries B.C (see Dispatches from Chechnya No. 12: The Fate of Chechnya's Architectural and Natural Treasures, http://www.idee.org/lreport12.html [accessed 31/05/08]).

Hopefully, the research currently being carried out will in time throw more light on the early period of the history of the region, but until then this brief overview will have to suffice, coupled with the clues about the ancient beliefs and practices of the Vainakh that can be gleaned from their stories.

***

Brave Näsni

There was once a man called Näsni. He was so timid that he hardly dared to go outside the house, and when a fly flew past he would crawl under his bed-cover. But once when he had to go out, he did not forget to take his sabre with him, and he made such tremendous passes in the air with it that he accidentally killed three flies. He was so proud of this that he had the following inscription engraved on his sabre: "This is the sabre of Näsni with which he slew sixty-three Narts from Erchustoj." Then he girt on his sabre, took a bag of flour on his back and set out on his travels.

Who knows how far he travelled? He went on, at any rate, till he came to a pear tree standing in a ravine; there he stopped, dug his sack of flour into the ground, and lay down to sleep. But all at once seven brothers of the Erchustojer Narts seemed suddenly to have sprung out of the earth and to stand a little distance away from him. They were wondering among themselves who this stranger could possibly be who had dared to penetrate into their country - for when a bird even flew over any of their lands it threw a feather down as a toll, and every four-footed animal passing through left a hoof or a paw. Then the youngest of the Narts crept softly up to the sleeping man, looked at his sabre, and then, returning to his brothers, told them of the inscription on it: "This is the sabre of Näsni with which he slew sixty-three Erchustojer Narts."

At that moment Näsni woke up. He saw the seven giants coming towards him and heard them say he must show them his powers. He showed them his sabre, and stamped his foot heavily on the place where he had buried his sack of flour so that a great cloud of flour rose in the air. "Look at that! That is what I am! When I even tread on the earth, great clouds of dust rise up." Then the Narts asked him to stay and live with them, for they had never seen such a man as he was, they would give him their sister as wife and half of all their possessions. Näsni did not dare to refuse this offer, and went with them. They built him a house, gave him their sister to wife, and Näsni lived with the Narts.

But presently a rhinoceros appeared in the wood: from time to time it came into the village and ate the people. The Narts determined to make war on this monster and sent for Näsni, asking him to come with them. But that did not suit him at all, and their messenger came back with the message that Näsni had no intention of going with them on the hunt. But … his wife forced her husband to go; she simply drove him out of the house. Näsni ran into the wood and climbed up a great pear tree, to hide himself there. But to his dismay, the rhinoceros spent the night right under this tree. The Erchustojer Narts, thinking that Näsni had already gone to the hunt, went themselves to the wood, met the rhinoceros and wounded it. The beast ran to its lair under the pear tree on which Näsni was still sitting. This hero fainted from terror, fell down right on the back of the rhinoceros, came to his senses again and held fast to the animal's hair. The rhinoceros was frightened too when it felt this unusual movement on its back, and rushed away straight to the village where the Narts lived. They took their weapons and shot it dead. Näsni behaved as if he was indignant at that. He cried, "Why have you killed it? It would have been more intelligent if you had noticed how I had tamed it." And the Narts believed he had really told the truth.

Some time later an enemy force came and wanted to fight with the Narts. They sent for Näsni again, and again the messenger came back with a refusal. But his wife fetched herself a big stick and drove her husband out of the house. Näsni went to the Narts' drove of horses, to seek the quietest animal he could find, and make good his escape on it. But none of the horses would let him come near them, they all kicked out at him. At last he did find an old mare, hobbled by the feet. He pricked her flanks with two little sticks, she stood it and did not stir. "This is my chance!" cried Näsni, got upon her back and rode away, but not in the direction of the enemy. When the Narts heard of it, they thought, "Ah! He is playing the same game as with the rhinoceros. He will come in good time," and so in this belief they closed with the enemy. But when Näsni's mare heard the shooting, she was a changed creature. She turned round like a shot and set off at full speed in the direction of the fighting.

Näsni had long since lost all control of her. In his fright he caught hold of the branches of a big plane tree, but the mare was galloping at such a rate that the whole tree came away in Näsni's hands. And the mare tore right into the heat of the battle, trampled the enemy with her hoofs, and all that were left Näsni struck with his plane tree or the Narts killed. When it was all over, the Narts took Näsni's mare by the bridle and led it home with songs of victory. Then they made Näsni their chief and he lives with them to this day (taken from Dirr. A. (1925) *Caucasian*

> *Folk-tales*, translated into English by Lucy Menzies, London & Toronto: J.M. Dent & Sons Ltd.).

Näsni, like all Chechen men, would have taken great pride in his sabre. And the inscription he had engraved on it clearly represents his attempt to live up to society's expectations of him.

> A good quality sword, such as the *tersmayla* swords ... would be treasured as a family heirloom ... the usual test for a good-quality kinzhal was to chop a large nail in two at one blow and to stab a thick copper-piece through with one thrust, and then to check the edge and point to ensure that they were undamaged. A good tersmayla sword was said to be able to sever a cow's or young bull's head at one blow (Malsagov, 2007, p.4).

To give some indication of the value of such weapons, it is worth noting that "It took an armourer and his apprentice about two weeks to make a dagger and more than a month to forge a sabre" (Jaimoukha, 2005, p.166).

Unfortunately, however, in view of his timidity, Näsni is clearly far from being the stereotypical ideal.

What we tend to find in indigenous communities where shamanism is practised is that the prospective shaman is generally singled out in some way,

> sometimes from birth, by a physically distinguishing feature such as an extra finger, a harelip or a birthmark. By the same token, the stigmata may take the form of mental or nervous dysfunction. A child who, at puberty, has fainting fits will often be regarded as a prospective shaman. So, too, will the victim of epilepsy, hysteria or the so-called "Arctic sickness", a loss of mental balance said to come about through prolonged exposure to sub-zero temperatures and boundless snowscapes (Rutherford, 1986, pp.34-35).

In this story however, the only way Näsni can be said to have been singled out is by his failing to live up to the expectations placed upon him.

When there are no physical or mental peculiarities to set shamans apart from the other members of their community, to make them appear to be special and worthy of respect, they are under constant pressure to perform extraordinary feats which can be seen to exceed the powers of mere mortals, and the practice of trickery is a means of achieving this. The Eskimo angakok, for example, during the Sedna feast, would stab themselves with harpoons, previously having placed under their clothes bladders filled with blood (see Maddox, 2003, pp.51-52). That trickery was, and still is, practised by shamans is undeniable, but perhaps it can be justified if it produces effective results, and in the case of Näsni it undoubtedly does.

Riding has always been a part of the job of sheepherding in Chechnya and also enjoyed as a sport. Traditionally, Chechens were sheep farmers, with men living a semi-nomadic life accompanying the herds through mountain pastures. In the twentieth century, however, opportunities for education and urban employment grew, and many people chose to leave farming to work in the towns or cities, with oil refining becoming an important part of the Chechen economy, drawing many workers. Recreational riding features daring tricks on horseback, and is common among young people in the countryside.

That the horse should feature prominently in Chechen folklore is not surprising in a land where distances are great and habitations may be few and far between.

> The reliability of one's horse may mean the difference between life and death. The quality of a man's horse is also an expression of a young man's virility. The young men traditionally proved their virility by conducting raids to steal livestock, especially horses, from neighbouring groups (Malsagov, 2007, p.4).

However, Näsni, in addition to lacking courage, also shows himself to be deficient in horse-riding skills too. He goes to the Narts' drove of horses, but only to seek the quietest animal he can find – an old mare who can barely walk. In effect, Näsni can be said to epitomize everything a Chechen man should not be.

As has already been pointed out, the style of storytelling most frequently employed in both shamanic stories and in fairy tales is that of magic realism, in which although "the point of departure is 'realistic' (recognizable events in chronological succession, everyday atmosphere, verisimilitude, characters with more or less predictable psychological reactions) ... soon strange discontinuities or gaps appear in the 'normal,' true-to-life texture of the narrative" (Calinescu, 1978, p.386). In this tale the magic only comes into play once Näsni lies down to sleep and the seven brothers of the Erchustojer Narts suddenly spring out of the earth – in other words, after he enters a trancelike state.

The Nart sagas are a series of tales originating from the North Caucasus and they form the basic mythology of the tribes in the area. Some are simply stories, but some have value as creation myths and ancient theology. The first written account of the material was produced by the Kabardian author Shora Begmurzin Nogma (written in Russian 1835-1843, published posthumously in 1861). As for the Narts themselves, they are a race of giants and heroes.

Some motifs in the Nart sagas are shared by Greek mythology. For example, the story of Prometheus chained to Mount Kazbek or to Mount Elbrus is similar to the story of Pkharmat. These shared motifs are seen by some as indicative of an earlier proximity of the Caucasian peoples to the ancient Greeks, also shown in the myth of the *Golden Fleece,* in which Colchis is generally accepted to have been part of modern-day Georgia or Abkhazia. (adapted from Wikipedia, the free encyclopedia, http://en.wikipedia.org/wiki/Nart_sagas [accessed 9/6/08]).

The number seven, incidentally, has a special significance for the Chechens. It is said that "If a traveller digs holes, or casts stones along the way, not only his name, but the names of his seven forefathers will be mentioned in vain."

> The mention of the seven forefathers has a deep meaning. That is, a person himself is thanked for his or her good deeds, but for the bad deeds, the forefathers will be mentioned as well. But if the forefathers are often mentioned, one will shorten the life of his posterity, because the forefathers are ashamed of the bad behavior and they have to lie on the ground, their faces down. Throughout the history of Chechens, the forefathers never liked to boast; they would prefer that their descendants act and behave always with dignity (taken from Usmanov, L. (1999) 'The Chechen Nation: A Portrait of Ethical Features', http://amina.com/article/chech_nati.html [accessed 4/06/08]).

Seven is actually a mystic or sacred number in many different traditions. Among the Babylonians and Egyptians, there were believed to be seven planets, and the alchemists recognized seven planets too. In the Old Testament there are seven days in creation, and for the Hebrews every seventh year was Sabbatical too. There are seven virtues, seven sins, seven ages in the life of man, seven wonders of the world, and the number seven repeatedly occurs in the Apocalypse as well. The Muslims talk of there being seven heavens, with the seventh being formed of divine light that is beyond the power of words to describe, and the Kabbalists also believe there are seven heavens – each arising above the other, with the seventh being the abode of God. Although the cosmology, described in Creation Myths, will vary from culture to culture, the structure of the whole cosmos is frequently symbolized by the number seven too,

> which is made up of the four directions, the centre, the zenith in heaven, and the nadir in the underworld. The essential axes of

> this structure are the four cardinal points and a central vertical axis passing through their point of intersection that connects the Upper World, the Middle World and the Lower World. The names by which the central vertical axis that connects the three worlds is referred to include the world pole, the tree of life, the sacred mountain, the central house pole, and Jacob's ladder (Berman, 2007, p.45).

It is widely recognized in neo-shamanic circles that by attacking our fears in non-ordinary reality, we are better able to cope with them in this world, and this is what Näsni can be said to succeed in doing in this tale. So in this sense it is a story that can be used for healing purposes, one which achieves its impact through the use of humor.

The healing effect of such stories derives from their dramatic potential to induce a psychological effect – the way in which they can free the reader from a debilitating self-image by focusing his/her consciousness instead on a world of supernatural power. Additionally, through the use of narrative, shamans are able to provide their patients "with a language, by means of which unexpressed, and otherwise inexpressible, psychic states can be expressed" (Lévi-Strauss, 1968, p.198).

The *Shimchong: The Blind Man's Daughter* narrative (see Berman, 2007), which is still used in Korea in shamanic ceremonies, illustrates the therapeutic power of storytelling in that the "patient" was supposed to be healed precisely at the climax of the story when Old Man Shim opens his eyes and sees his long-lost daughter. We have no way of knowing whether *Brave Näsni* was ever used for similar purposes but it is a possibility that cannot be discounted, and there is nothing of course to stop it being used for this purpose by teachers or therapists in our own day and age.

It has long been known that if a patient is shown that his particular ailment is also a general problem – even a god's ailment – he is in the company of men and gods, and this knowledge can produce a healing effect. In ancient Egypt, for example, when a person was bitten by a snake, the priest/physician would recite the myth of Ra and his mother Isis to the patient. The god Ra stepped on a poisonous serpent hidden in the sand that his mother had made and was bitten by it. Knowing that he was threatened with death, the gods caused Isis to work a spell which drew the poison out of him. The idea behind the telling of the tale was that the patient would be so impressed by the narrative that it would work as a cure (see Jung, 1977, pp.102-103).

The history of religion can be seen as "a treasure house of archetypal forms from which the doctor can draw helpful parallels and enlightening comparisons for the purpose of calming and clarifying a consciousness that is all at sea" (Jung, 1968, p.33). The message conveyed through the adoption of such an approach is that if the figures we read about and identify with can overcome difficulties, then we can too. And of course contemporary shamanic tales such as *Bundles* (see Berman 2007) can achieve this effect just as well as the ancient stories can.

Tales have long played an important part in the repertoire of healers, who have of course not only told stories but made use of their patients' stories too: according to medical historians, it was only in the 19th century that doctors actually began to examine their patients' bodies in any detail.

> Before that time they would observe them loosely, occasionally take their pulse or inspect their tongue, or peer at their urine or stools. But mostly they relied on the patient's account of what had happened. Eliciting this detailed "history" of their illness, watching for inconsistencies or omissions, and trying to guess at the "true" meaning of what was said, all made medical diagnosis into a type of literary criticism. For a long time, medicine was all about *stories*, not only the patient's "history" and the doctor's "diagnosis", but also the mingling of these two narratives in the medical consultation (Helman, 2006, p.152).

Through the shamanic story, a mythic world can be constructed and symbolically manipulated to elicit and to transact emotional experiences for the patient. As Dow (1986) explains, symbols affect mind, mind affects body and a cure is thus produced by making use of metaphor (see Winkelman, 2000, pp.237-239).

It has been shown through an empirically controlled experiment that "merely telling a human subject about controllability duplicates the effects of actual controllability" (Seligman, 1975, p.48). In other words, when we are told a story, regardless of whether the events in it correspond to the actual state of affairs in the world of experience, it can have the same effect on us as if it were a part of the world of real experience (see Rennie, 1996, p.224). From this it can be seen that the human spirit is not wholly determined by its physical environment but contributes, through the imaginative generation of narrative, to the construction of its own determining environment.

The themes of "*sortie du temps*, or temporal dislocation, and of the alteration or the transmutation of space" (Eliade, 1981, p.10) appear over and over again in shamanic stories and they can be found in *Brave Näsni* too. Notice, for example, the use of the formulaic device of asking "Who knows how far he travelled?" We learn that "He went on, at any rate, till he came to a pear tree standing in a ravine." As for the significance of the ravine, not only can it traditionally provide a point of access to the Lower World, it can also represent the centre of the universe, where the World Tree or The Tree of Life stands. In *Brave Näsni*, this takes the form of a pear tree – not a tree one would expect to find used for this purpose, but one which produces sweet-tasting fruit, and that is in keeping with the light-hearted and humorous tone of the tale.

On the other hand, there could well be another reason why the storyteller chose to make it a pear tree, as it had associations for the Chechens that the majority of us are probably not familiar with:

The Circassians regard the pear-tree as the protector of cattle. So

> they cut down a young pear-tree in the forest, branch it, and carry it home, where it is adored as a divinity. Almost every house has one such pear-tree. In autumn ... the tree is carried into the house with great ceremony to the sound of music and amid the joyous cries of all the inmates, who compliment it on its fortunate arrival. It is covered with candles, and a cheese is fastened to its top. Round about it they eat, drink, and sing. Then they bid the tree good-bye and take it back to the courtyard, where it remains for the rest of the year, set up against the wall, without receiving any mark of respect (Frazer, 1993, p.119).

The worship of trees should come as no surprise as nothing could be more natural. "For at the dawn of history Europe was covered with immense primeval forests, in which the scattered clearings must have appeared like islets in an ocean of green" (Frazer, 1993, p.109). And just how serious that worship was in former times may be gathered, for example,

> from the ferocious penalty appointed by the old German laws for such as dared to peel the bark of a standing tree. The culprit's navel was to be cut out and nailed to the part of the tree till all his guts were wound about its trunk. The intention of the punishment clearly was to replace the dead bark by a living substitute taken from the culprit; it was a life for a life, the life of a man for the life of a tree (Frazer, 1993, p.110).

For those who believed (and those present-day pagans who still believe) the world in general is animate, trees and plants have souls just like our own, and they were thus (and still are by many) treated accordingly.

In cultures that have the conception of three cosmic regions – those of Heaven, Earth and Hell – the "centre" constitutes the point of intersection of those regions. It is here that the break-through on to another plane is possible and, at the same time, communication between the three regions (Eliade, 1991, p.40). It is also generally accepted that

> The most widely distributed variant of the symbolism of the Centre is the Cosmic Tree, situated in the middle of the Universe, and upholding the three worlds as upon one axis. Vedic India, ancient China and the Germanic mythology, as well as the "primitive" religions, all held different versions of this Cosmic Tree, whose roots plunged down into Hell, and whose branches reached to Heaven" (Eliade, 1991, p.44).

So what at first sight might appear to be an insignificant fruit tree, now takes on a great deal more significance. Instead or referring to Hell and Heaven though, as Eliade does, it would be more accurate to label them the Lower and Upper Worlds, for in the case of so-called "primitive" religions, they were not necessarily black and white in the way that Eliade pictured them.

The ancient Chechen people thought that the Universe consisted of three worlds: the upper world – the world of God, the lower world – the world of spirits, and the Earth– the human world. These three worlds were believed to be interconnected, and it was the function of man to maintain and support this interconnectivity. The three worlds can be compared to three abstract circles: The first and the second are situated vertically and the point of their contact is the centre of the third one, the Earth circle, which is situated horizontally. Their common centre is known as the hearth cavity (*tush* in Chechen), to which man is believed to be directly connected. It is interesting to note that the capital of the Ancient Eastern State of Urartu was called Tushpa, which translates into English as "the artery of the hearth", and it was called this as it was regarded as the centre of the Universe at that time. Within this cosmological system, all essence – animal, mineral or vegetable – was considered to be of divine origin, and was expected to be treated with both care and respect. Understanding this is said to have enabled the forefathers to live in harmony with nature (see Usmanov, L. (1999) 'The Chechen Nation: A Portrait of Ethical Features', *http://amina.com/article/chech_nati.html* [accessed 4/06/08]).

To this day, the Chechen people think that all mankind is united in a blood kinship system, and that although the people of many nations are different in their languages, customs, and ceremonies, these are considered to be secondary matters.

> All people have physical needs, sorrow and joy, birth and death, and everybody is equal before them. ... There is nothing in nature and in society that man can look at with superiority. Chechen proverbs and tales teach a child to respect all living beings and nature. There is nothing unimportant in life: As the saying goes, "if you leave a peg in the ground, you'll have a headache, if you kill a frog, a cow will die, if you catch a butterfly, your sister will lose her joy of heart", etc. The Chechen people gather honey without killing the bees. They milk a cow with one hand, while supporting her udder with the other hand. ... Everything in life is useful, and if today, you think that something is useless and unnecessary, tomorrow it may be a vital necessity (Usmanov, L., 1999, 'The Chechen Nation: A Portrait of Ethical Features', http://amina.com/article/chech_nati.html [accessed 4/06/08]).

"Tales of power" have been defined as conscious verbal constructions based on numinous experiences in non-ordinary reality, "which guide individuals and help them to integrate the spiritual, mythical, or archetypal aspects of their internal and external experience in unique, meaningful, and fulfilling ways" (Kremer, 1988, p.192). And *Brave Näsni* very much fits into this category, being a tale of power that achieves its effect through the use of humor.

***

One of the neighboring regions, and bordering Chechnya, is Ingushetia, the second smallest republic of the Russian Federation. It was created in June 1992 as a result of the secession of the Ingush from Checheno-Ingushetia, where the Ingush had been very much in the minority. The decision to break away followed the declaration of independence by the Chechens in 1991. The partition left the Ingush without an urban centre, as all the cultural and educational facilities remained in Chechnya's capital Djohar (formerly Grozny) and the former capital of Ingushetia, Nazran, was unsuitable for the purpose. So a new capital, Magas, was inaugurated in 1998 (see Matveena, 1999, pp.91 & 92).

The information in the notes that follow is largely adapted from a 1997 paper by Johanna Nichols at the University of California, Berkeley, entitled 'The Ingush (with notes on the Chechen): Background information'.

"Ingush" is not the self-designation but a Russian ethnonym based on the name of the village Angusht (renamed in 1859 to Tarskaya and now part of North Ossetia). However, the indigenous Ingush, a people of Vainakh ancestry, call themselves Ghalghaaj (historically the name of a clan confederation).

Ingushetia remains one of Russia's poorest and most restive regions, having been destabilized by the ongoing military conflict in neighbouring Chechnya, a number of high-profile crimes, anti-government protests, terrorist attacks believed to have been carried out by Russian security forces, military excesses and a deteriorating human rights situation. However, since the beginning of the war between Georgia and Russia over South Ossetia, which broke out in August 2008, the number of attacks and abductions of Ingush civilians by "unknown" forces has fallen dramatically, and this could well be due to the fact that the majority of Russian forces were transferred to North and South Ossetia to deal with the conflict with Georgia instead.

Chechen and Ingush belong to the Nakh branch of the Nakh-Daghestanian, or Northeast Caucasian, language family. Despite being distinct languages, they are so similar that a Chechen will address an Ingush in Chechen, the Ingush will reply in Ingush, and they will both understand each other. Although orthographies using the Russian alphabet make it possible for these oral languages to be written down, for most people the chief vehicle of literacy is Russian. And if the Chechen and Ingush economies continue to be destroyed and unemployment and mass homelessness continue to undermine the social structure, there is danger that both Chechen and Ingush will only be used in the home and that much of the cultural heritage of the region will be lost as a result.

As for religion, the people were mostly pagan until the Russian conquest began, but then from the 17th to the early 19th centuries the Chechen and then the Ingush expressed their resistance by converting to Islam, and today they are Sunni Muslims. Two lay Sufi orders, the Q'ejla *tuobagh murdazh* (cited here in the Ingush form; generally known as Naqshbandiya) and Husien *hazhi murdazh* (Qadiri), are active in Ingushetia, as they are in Chechnya, and are credited with having helped keep Islam alive during the Soviet years.

Chechen-Ingush society has always been egalitarian, unstratified, and classless. Traditionally there was no formal political organization and no political or economic ranking, and the people were subdivided into a small number of tribes, each comprising a number of clans. Clans were exogamous, territorially compact groups and each was headed by a respected elder.

Clans continue to exist and they still determine social relationships and social behavior even today. An individual bears to all members of a clan the same social relationship that he or she bears to a relative in that clan; for instance, a man shows to all female members of his mother's clan the same deference and formality that he would show to his mother's older sister.

Traditionally, an Ingush or Chechen man is expected to know the names and birthplaces or origins of his paternal ancestors going back seven generations, once again an indication of the importance attached to the number seven, which appears over and over again in the folktales from the region. This tradition, which is not uniquely Chechen-Ingush but generally North Caucasian, means, incidentally, that there can be no genuine large-scale territorial disputes in the North Caucasus, since all parties know whose ancestors lived on what land.

The Ingush tale that follows is about a hero testing the infidelity of his friends, ending up in the lower world and overcoming a sarmak, and was found in the British Library in Malsagov, A.O. (2007) *Tales and Legends of the Ingush and Chechens,* translated from the Russian by D.G. Hunt. It was recorded in 1977 in the Ingush language from an unknown source in the village of Ojairakh and is from the private archive of I.A.Dakhkilgov.

The Strong Young Fellow

A father and a mother had a son of inordinate strength. He used to play with mountains, make waves in the seas, and he gave people no peace. The father and mother did not love their son, because he kept all the people in fear.

One day his mother pretended to be ill and she said to her son, "Beyond seven mountains lives a yeshap. Bring me some beans from his garden".

The young fellow set off to fulfil his mother's request. He cut across the seven mountains, and from the yeshap's garden he collected a sack full of beans. Then he beat up the yeshap, sat on him, and rode off home on him.

The people thought that the young fellow had perished. When they saw him riding on the yeshap, they all got a fright. "Vay, Moslems, help! The young fellow is riding on the yeshap!" And they all rushed in all directions.

They began to beg him to take the yeshap away. The young

fellow gave the yeshap a kick and drove him away.

The mother saw that the yeshap had done nothing to her son and she said, "Beyond seven mountains and beyond seven seas there is a forest guarded by a sarmak (A *sarmak* is a worm or a dragon that usually lies in wait by a river or a spring, only allowing people to take water if, in exchange, he is offered a girl as a sacrifice). Only on a fire of firewood from that forest can these beans be boiled".

The young fellow set off for the firewood. After a month he came back with the firewood and riding on the sarmak. The people became even more frightened, and they began to beg him to leave their region, together with the sarmak.

The young fellow realised that the people did not like him, and he went off, following his nose. On the road he met and made friends with two men. They began to live together. One day two of them went off hunting, while the youngest stayed home to prepare food for their return. The youngest one cooked the food and sat down to wait for the older ones.

At that time a dwarf the size of a lokot and with a beard the size of two lokots called on him. "Give me something to eat!" said he. The youngest one gave the guest a little food. The guest became angry, he tore a hair from his beard, tied up the youngest one with it, ate all of the prepared food, and left. The two elder ones arrived, and they ask, "Have you cooked some food for us?"

"It was cooked, but all the flies and the horse-flies ate it up", answered the youngest one.

On the second day the middle one was left at home, and the two others went off hunting. The middle one prepared the food. As on the first day, the dwarf with the beard came, he tied up the middle one with a hair from his beard, ate everything and left.

On the third day the turpal-hero stayed home. He had only just prepared the food when the dwarf with the beard came in. He wanted to tie up the turpal-hero like the two others, but the hero struck him with his sword and wounded him. The dwarf crawled away with difficulty. The two came back from hunting and the young fellow said to them, "Now I know who ate up the food that you prepared".

The friends decided to kill the evil dwarf, and they followed his trail. At the end of the earth they saw an opening. They took a long rope and decided to descend into it. The youngest one began to descend, but he got frightened, jerked the rope, and they quickly pulled him out. The middle one began to descend, he got frightened, jerked the rope, and they quickly pulled him out too. The hero said, "However much I jerk the rope, do not raise me, but continue to lower me".

He descended on to the roof of a certain house and saw a sleeping man who was guarding three beautiful girls. The hero cut off his head and decided to go up with the three sisters into the upper world. At first he began to raise the girls. The friends lifted the three sisters, but when they were lifting the hero, they cut through the rope and he fell down below. There he met a girl who said, "On the meadow, three rams are grazing. If you grab the white one by the leg, then you will find yourself in the upper world; the black one, and you will land up in the lower world; and the grey one, and you will stay here".

The hero seized the black ram by the leg and found himself in the lower world. There he asks people, "What does it mean: there is not a drop of water here? How do you live?"

The people say, "By the spring lies a sarmak, and we cannot free ourselves from him".

The hero came to the spring and saw the sarmak, one jaw of whom was resting against the sky, and the other on the ground. The sarmak started pouring flames over the hero. With a stroke of his sword the hero clove apart the sarmak's jaw, set his sword in him and went away.

Each person claimed this act as his own. "All right", said the hero then, "let the one who killed the sarmak pull out the sword that is set in him". But nobody was able to even move the sword. Then the hero easily plucked out the sword and asked that the people should help him to ascend to the upper world.

"On the high plane tree sits a falcon", they told the hero. "He can raise you into the upper world".

The falcon said to the hero, "Because you killed the sarmak, I will lift you into the upper world, but you must slaughter nine buffaloes, prepare the meat, and gather water in their skins. I will say 'Tsik!' and you give me a drink of water, I will say 'Kak!' and you give me meat".

They fly and fly, and the hero's meat and water came to an end. For the final time the falcon said "Tsik!", and the hero plucked out his eye and gave it to the falcon, the falcon said "Kak!", and he tore off the calf of his leg and gave it to the falcon. "That last piece of meat was tasty", said the falcon.

"That was the calf of my leg".

"Climb into my beak".

The hero crawled in, and the falcon spat him out alive and whole, and brought him to the upper world.

The hero killed his former friends, married one of the girls and began to live sweetly.

Gukgi-bulgi* to them.

White cattle to us.

***

*Gulgi-bulgi is used to express loss while white cattle represent abundance and wealth.

***

Although magic realism is the favored style of writing for the majority of shamanic stories, in this particular example of the genre there is hardly any preamble, and it is clear right from the second sentence that this is a tale about other realities: "A father and a mother had a son of inordinate strength. He used to play with mountains, make waves in the seas, and he gave people no peace".

Right from the outset the hero is marked out as being special and different in some way, which is of course what the prospective future shaman was required to be, and the suggestion that he is gifted with special powers is reinforced on the journey by what happens along the way.

Once again, as is so often the case in stories from the region, the numbers seven and three feature prominently. Our hero is sent on a journey "beyond seven mountains and beyond seven seas", and there are three companions, three beautiful girls, and three rams too.

The dwarf "the size of a lokot" and with a beard the size of two lokots", might well be an Atzan.

> According to some legends, the Atzans, a race of midgets, were forerunners of the giant Narts. [The Nart epics, which hold an important place in North Caucasian folklore, were probably formed over a period of 2000 years, beginning in Scythian times (800-700 B.C.] According to others, they were contemporaries, and had close and peaceful relations. They hunted on the same ground and, according to the mountain customs, they shared their kill. They were so small that they could easily walk along the stem of a fern and cut off the branches as they went. In spite of their size, the Atzans were wide-chested and broad-shouldered. They displayed great physical power, bravery, and courage. Anyone of them could, for example, while on the hunt, lift onto his shoulders and carry to camp his killed game – aurochs and mountain goat. In addition, they were unsurpassed runners (Benet, 1974, p.97).

As for the significance of the three rams in the tale, the animal of course plays an important part in the story of the Golden Fleece. It is said that in ancient Greece a ram with a fleece of gold opened his lips and speaking with the voice of a man warned the children of the first wife of Athamas, whose name was Nephele, of the danger they were in from his second wife, whose name was Ino, who was plotting their death.

> So they mounted the ram and fled with him over land and sea. As they flew over the sea, the girl slipped from the animal's back, and falling into water was drowned. But her brother Phrixus was brought safe to the land of Colchis, where reigned a child of the Sun. Phrixus married the King's daughter, and she bore him a son Cytisorus. And there he sacrificed the ram with the golden fleece to Zeus the God of flight (Frazer, 1993 p. 290).

The idea of the ram being used as a vehicle to access other worlds is thus not unfamiliar to the peoples of the region.

Of the three companions, our hero proves to be the only one brave enough to descend through the opening in the earth by means of the rope so as to kill the evil dwarf. He also proves to be the only person able to kill the sarmak who stops the people there from obtaining water to drink. In return the people put our hero in contact with the falcon who can take him back to the upper world, where the three beautiful girls and the two companions who were responsible for leaving him stranded in the lower world are to be found.

Descending by means of a rope through an opening in the earth is of course a traditional means of accessing the lower world when journeying into non-ordinary reality, the spring represents a place of power which needs to be reactivated by removing the sarmak so that equilibrium can be restored to the community once again, and by bringing this about our hero is in fact fulfilling the traditional role played by the shaman.

In the tales of the Vainakhs (the collective local name of the

> Ingush and Chechens) the idea of three worlds is met quite often. The hero of a tale and of epic poetry lands up in the lower world and there continues to accomplish the heroic deeds that he accomplishes in the sunlit (upper) world. In the underground world the positive hero meets three sisters (daughters of a prince or *padchakh*) kidnapped by an evil monster; he fulfils their mission and frees them from misfortune. The role of the evil monster is performed by a dragon (*sarmak*), [reminding us of the eristic nature of what is in effect shamanic journeying] and that of the hero's [spirit] helper is [played by] the eagle (*erzi*). (Malsagov, 2007, p.260).

In *The Strong Young Fellow* however, the eagle is replaced by a falcon. The falcon is a symbol of liberty, freedom, and victory. Therefore, it also symbolizes hope to all those who are in bondage whether moral, emotional, or spiritual. Moreover, in early Egyptian hieroglyphs the falcon represented the word for "god". It was associated with sky deities, who may have had falcons' heads. In early dynasties, the king's ascension was known as the "Flight of the Falcon". A human-headed falcon was a symbol of the human soul. The falcon helped cure the soul and escorted the soul back to the world of souls. And in *The Strong Young Fellow,* the falcon takes the hero from the Lower World back to the world of souls.

The same theme can be found in other folktales from the region – *Chaitong, the Son of a Bear,* for example, the third story in *Tales of the Inguish and Chechens*. Chaitong has to feed the eagle that helps him to ascend to the Upper World with his own flesh too when he runs out of meat and bread – with the calves of both his legs, and the muscle of his arm

As has already been noted, the death/rebirth cycle, as is the case with every other detail of the shaman's calling, shows regional variations so that in some places it is reduced to the symbolical form of an initiatory rite. In others, the extreme opposite applies and the candidate may have to undergo ordeals of an extremely painful nature, either self-inflicted or inflicted by initiators (Rutherford, 1986, p.38). In this particular story, the ordeal entails the prospective shaman feeding the falcon with parts of his own body.

> [T]he mythology and the rites of magical flight peculiar to shamans and sorcerers confirm and proclaim their transcendence in respect to the human condition: by flying into the air, in bird form or in their normal human shape, shamans as it were proclaim the degeneration of humanity. For … a number of myths refer to a primordial time when *all human beings* could ascend to heaven, by climbing a mountain, a tree, or a ladder, or flying by their own power, or being carried by birds. The degeneration of humanity henceforth forbids the mass of mankind to fly to heaven; only death restores men (and not all of them!) to their primordial condition; only then can they ascend to heaven, fly like birds, and so forth (Eliade, 1989, p.480).

The ability of our hero to be carried by the falcon from the lower world to the upper world thus singles him out as being different to others, in that he is shown to be able to transcend the human condition, which is one of the attributes that the shaman was traditionally noted for.

As for the conclusion to the tale, on his return to this reality, our hero (who, as is customary in tales from the Caucasus, is never given a name) kills the two companions who betrayed him, marries one of the girls and begins "to live sweetly", thus presumably no longer feeling any need to keep "all the people in fear" as he had previously done. In this way the threat to the community is removed and the shaman's journey is thus complete.

Chapter 4

Azerbaijan

Since olden times Azerbaijan has been called "Odlar Yurdu" – Land of Fires – because of the burning jets of natural gas escaping from the ground and the Zoroastrian practice of fire worship, and to this day in the village of Ramany near Baky one can still find the ancient temples of the fire-worshippers. More recently, as in the quote that follows, the country has been compared to an eagle:

> The soul of our people is pained and crying because our 'eagle' [the shape of Azerbaijan on a map] is desperately trying to survive the countless attacks targeting our bird. But never forget that an eagle is the kind of all birds. A day will come when our eagle will be healed, and then we will soar high with dignity, power and grace. (Natalya Ahmadova, Baku recipient of a U.S. Freedom Support scholarship, studying at La Porte High School in La Porte, TX, taken from *Azerbaijan International* (5.2) Summer 1997.)

Either way, it is a land full of contrasts, from its various geographical features to its Cultural mix of East and West, as will soon become apparent.

Azerbaijan, the largest of the three main Caucasian nations, is bordered by Russia on the north, Georgia on the northwest, Armenia on the west, Iran on the south, and the Caspian Sea on the east. Much of the country is mountainous, with The Greater Caucasian range rising to the north, below which lies the Kura-Araz lowland. The total area of the Azerbaijan Republic, including the Nakhchivan Autonomous Republic, is 86,000 square kilometres. However, the most remarkable geographical feature of

Azerbaijan must surely be its variety, with it being possible to travel within a day from the hot lowlands of the dry subtropics to everlasting snows and glaciers in the mountains. In fact, within the one country, can be found nine of the thirteen climatic zones that exist in the world, with the climate ranging from +45° C in the plains to -45° C in the mountains (see Dragadze, 2000, pp.50-54).

Geographically vulnerable yet rich in resources, the country has been buffeted and badgered through the ages by invaders attempting to impose their own ways on the people – by tsars and shahs, caliphs and khans, by Persian Achaemenians (4th century B.C.), Arabs (7th century A.D.), and Mongols (12-13th century), right through to the Russians, and some would say, in the present day and age, by the Armenians too (referring to the political impasse over the status of Nagorno-Karabakh).

Azerbaijan has been inhabited for at least 3000 years, and probably a lot longer than that. Some theories even place the Garden of Eden in southern Azerbaijan (now part of Iran). Scythians settled in the area in the 9th century BC, followed by the Medes, followers of Zoroastrianism. The Archaemenid Persians took over half the country 200 years later. Azerbaijan's decision to back Alexander the Great's attack on Persia in 330 BC meant that it drifted into the Seleucid then Parthian empires, which fought interminable wars with the Romans, who finally marched all the way to Qobustan in 66BC. By the 4th century the area had been extensively Christianized.

With a series of Muslim-Arab invasions and the arrival of several waves of Turkic tribes (the ancestors of today's Azerbaijanis) that soon changed. Beginning around 1050, the country enjoyed a cultural renaissance, and achieved many of its greatest architectural and artistic achievements. However, this was crushed by the brutal arrival of various Mongol and Central Asian armies, from Genghis Khan to Tamerlane.

Following centuries saw a three-way struggle between Russia, Turkey and Persia that finally ended in 1828, when Russia and

Persia definitively divided Azerbaijan along the Araz River, with the south of what was then Azerbaijan remaining in Iran. During the period of Russian rule, many Armenian Christians emigrated from their traditional lands in (what is now) eastern Turkey to the relative safety of the Russian empire, creating a future political time bomb in the Nagorno-Karabakh region where they slowly came to form a majority. Meanwhile, Azerbaijan's economy grew in relation to Russia's. In the middle of the 19th century the region was a participant in the birth of the modern petroleum industry, with Azerbaijan providing Russia (and later the Soviet Union) with crude oil, chemicals, textiles, food and wine.

During 1988, with Gorbachev preaching perestroika and Soviet power waning, Nagorno-Karabakh's now-majority Armenian population started demanding a transfer to Armenia. Azerbaijan reacted heavy-handedly by removing Nagorno-Karabakh's autonomous status that had been previously granted to it by Stalin. A spiral of communal attacks then developed into a general conflict, with Azeri-Armenians and Armenian-Azeris fleeing their homes wherever they were in the minority, fearing ethnic violence. What followed in Nagorno–Karabakh was virtually a full-scale war. Not only did the conflict result in thousands of casualties, but also the creation of about one million refugees. Although a cease-fire in 1994 stemmed the worst of the violence, the situation still remains far from resolved. Some 15% of Azerbaijan remains under Armenian occupation. Nagorno-Karabakh has declared itself a republic and has little interest in giving back any territory to Azerbaijan, who can be said to have come out of the conflict worse off than their neighbors.

After a very shaky war-torn period of independence from the Soviet Union, Azerbaijan's stability was restored by the iron hand of its wily old Soviet-era ruler, Heydar Aliyev. His ability to pull the country together again won him hero status locally, though his lip service to democracy did not encourage similar admiration abroad, nor did the legally dubious transition of power that he arranged to his son. For Western investors however, who built the multi-billion oil-pipeline to Turkey (via Georgia) that was completed in 2006, Azerbaijan's stability counted for more than the niceties of election transparency. As to how much the nation benefits from the potential export opportunities the pipeline affords, it will depend a lot on how much institutional corruption is allowed to siphon off the revenues, and that remains to be seen (adapted from www.lonelyplanet.com/worldguide/azerbaijan/history [accessed 15/4/08]).

Each year the American Bureau of Democracy, Human Rights, and Labor release an International Religious Freedom Report on Azerbaijan and it provides a useful source for an overview of the current situation in the country. The following information is taken from the 2007 report.

The report notes that although the Constitution provides that persons of all faiths may choose and practice their religion without restriction, in practice there were both some abuses and restrictions. Some religious groups reported delays in and denials of registration; as in previous years, there continued to be some limitations upon the ability of groups to import religious literature, and local officials at times harassed and detained members of "non-traditional" religious groups. There were also some reports of societal abuses or discrimination based on religious belief or practice. There was popular prejudice against Muslims who convert to other faiths, and hostility towards groups that proselytize, particularly evangelical Christian and other missionary groups.

According to official figures, out of a total population of 8.5 million, approximately 96 percent of the people are Muslim. The remainder of the population consists mostly of Russian Orthodox, Armenian Orthodox, Jews, and nonbelievers. Among the Muslim majority, religious observance is relatively low, and Muslim identity tends to be based more on culture and ethnicity than religion. As for Christians living in Azerbaijan, the vast majority are

Russian Orthodox whose identity, like that of Muslims, tends to be based as much on culture and ethnicity as religion. Shi'a, Sunni, Russian Orthodox, and Jews are considered to be the country's "traditional" religious groups, though small congregations of Lutherans, Roman Catholics, Baptists, Molokans (Russian Orthodox Old Believers), Seventh-day Adventists, and Baha'is have been present for more than 100 years.

There is also a small but strong current of Zoroastrian beliefs in evidence left over from Azerbaijan's pre-Islamic days. Practised mostly in the countryside, its followers believe that there is only one god, Ahura Mazda, the Lord of Wisdom. They are best known for their temples, which contain naturally occurring fire due to the oil rising from the earth (see Kaeter, 2004, p.90).

As for the status of religious freedom, the law expressly prohibits the Government from interfering in the religious activities of any individual or group; however, there are exceptions, including cases where the activity of a religious group "threatens public order and stability." Since 2001 religious groups have been required to be registered by the Government (the SCWRA) but registration, the report notes, is burdensome, and there have been frequent, sometimes lengthy, delays in obtaining registration, in particular for a number of Protestant Christian groups. Some groups characterized the seven-step application process as arbitrary and restrictive. As for unregistered organizations, they are vulnerable to allegations that they are illegal and as a result subject to attacks and closures by local authorities, which makes it difficult for them to function.

Restrictions on religious freedom are evident in the country. For example, the law on religious freedom expressly prohibits religious proselytizing by foreigners, and the Government strictly enforces this. The Government is concerned about Islamic missionary groups (predominantly Iranian and Wahhabi) operating in the country and continues to restrict their activities. Some Muslims complained about the SCWRA's allegedly indiscriminate use of the term "Wahhabi" to cast a shadow on devout Muslims. Local Protestant Christians also claimed that SCWRA Chairman Orujov derogatorily referred to their organizations as "sects". During the reporting period, there were several incidents of police arresting Wahhabis and sometimes confiscating weapons and literature, particularly in the northern regions of Guba, Khachmaz, Gax, and Zaqatala, according to local contacts and the press.

Abuses of religious freedom have also been noted in the report, with "non-traditional" religious groups facing particularly acute problems operating in remote regions of the country, including the exclave of Nakhchivan. Despite their being fewer incidents than in previous years of official harassment, interruptions of religious services, or police intimidation and fines, such incidents still continued, and there were reports of beatings during police raids. Government authorities also tried to restrict what they claimed were political and terrorist activities by Iranian and other clerics operating independently of the organized Muslim community, and there were reports that the Government harassed such Muslim groups based on security concerns – alleged links to terrorism.

Societal abuses and discrimination are still in evidence too, with hostility between Armenians and Azerbaijanis, intensified by the Nagorno-Karabakh conflict, remaining strong. In those areas of the country controlled by Armenians, all ethnic Azerbaijanis have fled, and the mosques that had not been destroyed remained inactive. Animosity towards ethnic Armenians elsewhere in the country forced most of them to depart between 1988 and 1990, and all Armenian churches, many of which were damaged in ethnic riots that took place more than a decade ago, remained closed. As a consequence, the estimated 10,000 to 30,000 ethnic Armenians who remained were unable to attend services in their traditional places of worship.

An additional problem noted in the report is that newspapers and television broadcasts continue to depict "non-traditional" religious groups as threats to the identity of the nation and as undermining the country's traditions of interfaith harmony, and this leads to local harassment.

What we can conclude from this is that although in Azerbaijan all religious communities are equal in theory, it would seem that some are clearly more equal than others, and this would appear to be the case in other countries that were formerly part of the Soviet Union too. One of the results of the collapse of Communism was more religious freedom, but there was also a growing sense of frustration among the people caused by their inability to make effective use of their new-found freedom to take control of their lives. The New Religious Movements were blamed by the authorities for many of the problems that resulted from the changes, with the belief being encouraged in the media that a foreign invasion was in effect taking place, and this in turn led to new laws being introduced which not only made it difficult for the NRMs to obtain official recognition but also for their members to practice their faiths. The relative freedom that initially prevailed after the fall of Communism in the majority of the former Soviet states was followed by a reaction against the changes that had taken place by the authorities, supported in each case by the religious groups that happened to have been historically dominant prior to the formation of the Soviet Union.

Let us now consider what evidence remains of the paganism that was practised in former times in Azerbaijan, and also what remains of it in the form of festivals that are still celebrated today and in the beliefs of people, for the evidence for pagan survivals and their integration into new faiths goes beyond just literary sources.

Novruz Bayram (novruz means 'new day') is a widely celebrated holiday in Azerbaijan. It is an ancient public holiday of the new year and spring, celebrated at the equinox, usually on 21 March. People prepare for it well in advance, repairing their houses and apartments, sewing new clothes, painting eggs and germinating wheat on decorative plates. Various sweetmeats are prepared on the eve of the holiday, especially *govurga,* which contains sultanas and nuts, *pakhlava* and *shekerbura.* In the evening, bonfires are lit in the courtyards and children jump over them, while the adults prepare more food in the hope of a rich and fertile year ahead (Dragadze, 2000, p.36). Though not specifically shamanic, there is clear evidence that the holiday has pagan origins – the jumping over the bonfires, for example, as a means of moving from one world into another.

Then there is the observation among the Tatar of Azerbaijan of the "rites of spring." The Tatar of Azerbaijan, who number about 30.000, are a group of Turkic people who have substantial colonies in virtually every republic of the former Soviet Union. They speak a unique language called Kazan Tatar, although many now claim Russian as their mother tongue. They are a settled people, mostly peasants and merchants, who have completely lost their traditional tribal structure. Although the Tatar are primarily Islamic, many still observe *sabantuy,* or "rites of spring." This is an ancient pagan agricultural festival that is celebrated simultaneously with the anniversary of the founding of the Russian Tatar Republic on June 25, and the celebrations have their origins in shamanism (the belief in an unseen world of gods, demons, and ancestral spirits). Though many Tatar will identify themselves as Muslims before they will identify themselves as Tatar, at the same time they still honor saints and holy places, and some beliefs in supernatural powers such as the "evil eye" (the ability to curse someone with a glance) still exist from their pre-Islamic days.

As for the evidence of shamanism having been practised in the region,

> during the first centuries of the Christian era, Turkic tribes such as Bulgars, Savirs, Khazars and Huns played an ever growing role in the cultural and political life of the region. After the 4th century AD, Turkic folk medicine - shamanism, treatment with

magic and medicinal herbs - began to spread throughout Azerbaijan. Healers were named "Gam" (shamans) or "Otachi" (herbalists), while medicines were called "Ota" (from "ot" - herb). Later, the Turkic impact on Azerbaijani traditional medicine became even stronger. That is why folk medicine in medieval Azerbaijan is often called "Turkachara" (Türkəçarə – Turkic healing). During the 3rd-6th centuries, medical treatment related with Turkic shamanism was widespread among nomadic and semi-nomadic tribes of Azerbaijan such as Bulgar and Khazar. This was a healing method related to ritual dances and songs ("qam oyunu" in Azeri Turkic). Shamans (qam) used special ecstatic performances to expel malicious spirits from the diseased person's body. Such procedures could render a psychological or hypnotic effect and often really relaxed the patient, removed psychological tension and treated some nervous diseases. Musical accompaniment on tambourine and gopuz (a stringed instrument), and, sometimes, narcotic plants like henbane and fly agaric were applied to enhance the psychological effect. (taken from , www.alakbarli.aamh.az/index.files/10.htm [accessed 20/4/08]).

The Faithful Servant

Once upon a time there was a king who had three sons. Now he wanted to test them in order to find out which was the cleverest, and to that end he gave each of them five or six hundred roubles, saying; "Go and do what you like with the money, amuse yourselves well."

The two elder sons soon found friends with whom they spent the money in merry-making. The youngest sought for friends, but finding none to his mind determined to spend the money on something useful. He passed through a graveyard and saw there a man striking a grave with a stick [In the Caucasus, this is regarded as the greatest insult one can offer the dead]. He went up to the man and asked him why he did that. "The dead man who lies here owes me seventy roubles; that is why I insult his grave," answered the man. The king's son at once pulled out this sum, gave it to the man and told him he must stop his shameful conduct and leave the grave in peace. Then the king's son went home, but he was very much afraid at the thought of having to tell his father how he had spent his money. The other two brothers arrived at the same time from their merry-making.

Three days later the king called his sons to him, and asked them what they had done with their money and what adventures they had had. The two elder brothers told what a gay time they had had, and how they had spent their money. But the youngest told what had happened to him in the graveyard. "Except for these seventy roubles which I gave to the grave-spoiler, I have not spent anything. I have all the rest still," he added.

The king was very angry with his two elder sons: but he praised the youngest highly for his conduct, and promised that he should be king after his father died. "But for the present," he added, "you shall have your own house and as much money as you require. Get some things together and engage a servant; but only take a man who, when you say to him at dinner: 'Come here and dine with me,' refuses your invitation."

A few days later the youngest son went to the bazaar to seek for a servant. He found one, and that evening when he sat down to dinner he invited him to come and dine with him. The servant accepted the invitation, but the prince, who had not forgotten his father's advice, dismissed him the following day and engaged another. This one too, for the same reason, he had to part with at once. But the third refused the invitation to dine with his master in these words: "Dine, sir? I will dine on what is left over." And no matter how often the prince repeated his invitation, the servant remained firm and said only, "After you, sir." "This is the servant my father spoke of," said the prince to himself, "I will keep him." And he engaged him for a wage of seventy roubles.

And the servant was in truth both useful and clever, and the prince became very fond of him. After some time the prince collected a large party to journey into a neighbouring country. One or two merchants attached themselves to the party. Now there were two ways into that country, one took seven days, the other three months; but the shorter way invariably disappeared, no one knew where to. But in spite of that, the servant advised the prince to go by the shorter way. "But whoever travels by that road never returns!" said the prince. "There is no reason why you should trouble yourself about that," answered the servant, "I beg you to choose the shorter way." And the prince, who had a great affection for his servant, agreed to his request and let it be known that he had chosen to travel by the shorter way. The merchants who had attached themselves to his party begged him to alter his plans, but the prince kept to his resolve.

And so they set out. In the evening they pitched their camp at a certain place, had a meal and then lay down to rest. The servant kept watch. About midnight the prince's dog began to bark and the servant heard someone talking to it from behind a bush, "Here, dog, your master will probably kill you soon, and smear your blood on his eyes; let me take some of his goods." But the dog barked right on till morning, and the servant watched all that time.

In a short time they reached their destination successfully, sold their wares, bought new goods, and were finished with their business when those merchants who had chosen the long way arrived. They were not a little surprised that the prince's party had come through the short way unharmed. The servant invited them to attach themselves to the prince's party, at least for the homeward journey, and to travel by the short way. This time they agreed and all set out together.

It so happened that they pitched their camp one night at the same place where the prince's party had spent a night on the outward journey. When everyone was asleep and only the servant was on guard, the dog barked again at midnight, and again the servant heard a voice behind a bush: "Your master will soon kill you, and smear your blood on his eyes: let me take his goods." The servant wakened the prince and told him how he heard a voice, that he wanted to follow it, if the prince would come after him. "Very good," said the prince, "lead the way." So the servant went in the direction from which the voice had come, and soon saw a man who seemed to be running away. He ran after him, and noticed that the fugitive suddenly disappeared into the earth. On going nearer, he saw that there was a great hole in the ground. In the meantime the prince had come up and the servant said: "I am going to go down there; let a rope down and pull up whatever I tie on to it."

But when the servant had climbed down into the hole, he found whole rooms full of gold and silver with three maidens sitting in them, each more beautiful than the other. "Why have you come here?" they asked him; "all this belongs to the seven Divs. We belong to them too, and they brought each of us from a different part of the world. If they find you, they will eat you up." "Where are they, then?" asked the servant. "In that room." The servant went in, hewed the seven Divs to pieces and put their ears in a cloth. Then he took the maidens with him, bound them one after the other on to the rope, and the prince pulled them up. The servant collected all the gold and silver and everything he could find, tied it all on to the rope, and the prince pulled it up. Everything the Divs possessed they had taken from those who had travelled by the shorter way, and the travellers themselves they had killed.

When he had sent up everything, the servant tied the rope round himself and let himself be drawn up. Then the whole party set out on the homeward way after they had loaded their camels with the newly found treasure and with the three maidens.

When he arrived home, the prince found that his father had gone blind and his sister mad. All that had come to pass because those who stayed at home had been told that their youngest son and brother had chosen the shorter way, and that they might therefore regard him as lost. The father's eyes had lost their sight from incessant weeping, and from the heavy anxiety his sister's mind had given away.

After a time, however, the servant asked the prince to go hunting with him. They wandered about the whole day, but could find nothing. When they were on the way home in the depth of night, the servant killed the hound, took out his handkerchief and dipped it in the animal's blood. Then he said to the prince: "Do not be sad on account of the dog. What has happened, has happened; a misfortune is soon over." The prince said nothing out of love for his servant, and they went on homewards.

Two or three days later the servant came to his master and said: "My time is nearly up. You three brothers must now marry the three maidens we pulled out of the Div's pit." And so it was. The eldest son took the eldest maiden, the second son the second maid, and the youngest the youngest.

Shortly after that, the year for which the servant had engaged himself to the prince came to an end. The prince urged him to stay, but the servant would not agree, took his wages, and said: "Come, we will go for a walk, for I want to tell you something." They set out, and the servant turned towards the graveyard where before the man had insulted the grave. As they drew near they saw the light was shining out of the grave: it was a fresh grave, newly dug. The servant stepped into it with the words, "I will see if it fits me," laid himself down, and it fitted him exactly. The prince even said, "It looks as if that grave had been meant for you." "Give me your hand and help me out," said the servant, and when the prince stretched out his hand the servant laid in it his seventy-rouble wage and the blood-stained handkerchief, saying: "Smear the blood on your father's eyes; boil the Div's ears in water and give it to your sister to drink; then your father will recover his sight, and your sister her reason. Your father shall vacate the throne for you." And as he said that, his grave closed over him.

The prince mourned his servant and went sadly home. But he carried out his servant's orders; his father's eyes received back their sight, and his sister's reason was restored to her. And then the old king gave up the throne and his youngest son took it in his place, and reigned for the good of his people (taken from Dirr. A. (1925) *Caucasian Folk-tales*, translated into English by Lucy Menzies, London & Toronto: J.M. Dent & Sons Ltd.).

These are the notes Dirr provides on the origin of the tale: "An Udian tale – a small people with Lesghian tongue. They only inhabit two villages – Warthaschen and Nisch, east of Nuchi in Trans-Caucasia" [now Azerbaijan].

***

As in many folktales from the Caucasus, the numbers three and seven play a significant part in the tale. We are told that there are three sons, and that the king waits three days before summoning them. We then learn that it is the third servant tried out by the youngest son who turns out to be the right choice for the job, that the long route for the journey takes three months, and that there are three maidens being held captive. As for the number seven, the route recommended by the servant for the journey takes seven days and there are the seven Divs who feature in the tale too.

Pythagoras called three the perfect number in that it represented the beginning, the middle and the end, and he thus regarded it as a symbol of Deity. And the number three plays an important part in our tale. This repetition of the number must surely be more than just coincidental and we are led to conclude that this features in the tale for a purpose. A Trinity is not only found in Christianity, though given the fact that the Georgians are Orthodox Christians this must be the most likely reason for its inclusion in the tale, though the origin of the tale itself could well have preceded the advent of Christianity given its shamanic aspects. The importance of the number in our tale could well be the result of the influence of Christianity but it also refers to the three stages in the cycle of life and adds to the universality of the story's appeal. In fact, what we have in the tale is three times three, a trinity of trinities. The Pythagoreans believed that man is a full chord, or eight notes, and deity comes next. Three is the perfect trinity and represents perfect unity, twice three is the perfect dual, and three times three is the perfect plural, which explains why nine was considered to be a mystical number. Our tale certainly has a mystical element to it, and its connection to such symbolism clearly gives it greater significance. However, to suggest that the comparison with a trinity of trinities was intentional on the part of its author is perhaps, though interesting, a bit too far-fetched. One of the problems when it comes to considering symbolism is symbolic meaning can be read into almost anything and there is often no way of checking the interpretation.

As for the number seven, it is a mystic or sacred number in many different traditions. Among the Babylonians and Egyptians, there were believed to be seven planets, and the alchemists recognized seven planets too. In the Old Testament there are seven days in creation, and for the Hebrews every seventh year was Sabbatical too. There are seven virtues, seven sins, seven ages in the life of man, seven wonders of the world, and the number seven repeatedly occurs in the Apocalypse as well. The Muslims talk of there being seven heavens, with the seventh being formed of divine light that is beyond the power of words to describe, and the Kabbalists also believe there are seven heavens – each arising above the other, with the seventh being the abode of God.

Although the cosmology, described in Creation Myths, will vary from culture to culture, the structure of the whole cosmos is frequently symbolized by the number seven too,

> which is made up of the four directions, the centre, the zenith in heaven, and the nadir in the underworld. The essential axes of this structure are the four cardinal points and a central vertical axis passing through their point of intersection that connects the Upper World, the Middle World and the Lower World. The names by which the central vertical axis that connects the three worlds is referred to include the world pole, the tree of life, the sacred mountain, the central house pole, and Jacob's ladder (Berman, 2007, p.45).

It is the youngest son the king chooses to succeed him, the one who spends his money on stopping a grave-spoiler from defiling a grave. In other words, it is the son who shows respect for the traditions and customs of the community, and who is thus most likely to maintain them and ensure both its continuity and survival. And in the same way the youngest son makes his choice for a servant, based on the same principles as those used by his father – by selecting the person who shows he knows his place and will thus not upset the equilibrium of the community.

As an intermediary, the shaman can be said to serve as a bridge or a link – "to facilitate the changing of condition without violent social disruptions or an abrupt cessation of individual and collective life" (Van Gennep, 1977, p.48). And that is what the youngest son achieves by the end of the tale, with the assistance of his spirit helper.

Faced with the choice of which route to take, the youngest son puts his faith in his servant, who suggests the quicker but supposedly more dangerous route. In other words, he trusts in what can be regarded as the shamanic process, and it is his bravery in this respect that marks him out as being different to the rest.

This is what we tend to find in indigenous communities where shamanism is practised, that the prospective shaman is generally singled out in some way,

> sometimes from birth, by a physically distinguishing feature such as an extra finger, a harelip or a birthmark. By the same token, the stigmata may take the form of mental or nervous dysfunction. A child who, at puberty, has fainting fits will often be regarded as a prospective shaman. So, too, will the victim of epilepsy, hysteria or the so-called "Arctic sickness", a loss of mental balance said to come about through prolonged exposure to sub-zero temperatures and boundless snowscapes (Rutherford, 1986, pp.34-35)

In this particular story it is the youngest son's respect for tradition and bravery that indicate his suitability for his future role.

The Faithful Servant is very much a tale that focuses on healing, and what it shows is that among indigenous peoples, "all concern with health and curing is a religious transaction. If a person suffers from bad health, if he or she falls critically ill, it is all provided for by his or her relations with the supernatural world" (see Hultkrantz, 1992, p.1). Although minor injuries and illnesses such as coughs or colds may not be regarded in this light, generally speaking all disease is believed to have its origin in a disturbed relationship with the supernatural.

Not only has the shaman traditionally played the role of a healer as the youngest son does in this particular tale, but shamanic practices have also had a considerable influence on contemporary forms of healing.

> Specific techniques long used in shamanism, such as change in state of consciousness, stress-reduction, visualisation, positive thinking, and assistance from non-ordinary sources, are some of the approaches now widely employed in contemporary holistic

practice (Harner, 1990, p. xiii).

Jungian and Gestalt therapists also use guided visualization with their patients to enable them to access inner wisdom. This often involves the patient having a dialogue with an inner sage or teacher in which he/she is encouraged to ask whatever questions seem to be most helpful, and the process can be compared to the shaman's journey to find a spirit teacher (see Walsh, 1990, p.132).

According to Harner (1990), in shamanic terms illnesses, physical or mental, are not considered to be natural to the body and are usually viewed as power intrusions. To resist them you need to be in possession of guardian spirit power and serious illness is usually only possible when a person has lost this energizing force or it becomes depleted. Ingerman (1993), however, maintains there are three possible causes of illness – a person's power animal leaving without a new one taking its place, soul loss, or spirit intrusion. Cases of soul loss are believed to be the result of an emotional or physical trauma. To cope with such an experience, a piece of our life force is said to separate from the body and travel into non-ordinary reality. In psychological terms this is known as *dissociation*. Another cause of soul loss could be the theft of part of our life force by another person.

Vinogradov (2002) points out how classical shamans among Southern Siberian ethnic groups "always use the spiritual context/vocabulary of a particular culture" and the same observation can be applied to the way indigenous shamans work in other parts of the world too. In other words, as Vinogradov goes on to add, "they are not Universalists like Jungian analysts [or neo-shamanic practitioners], but ... deeply embedded in their [own] cultures and their myths." Moreover, their folktales (and rituals), as we see here with the smearing of a sacrificed animal's blood used as a cure, reflect this.

According to Eliade, "the shaman is indispensable in any ceremony that concerns the experiences of the human soul [when it is seen as] ... a precarious psychic unit, inclined to forsake the body and an easy prey for demons and sorcerers" (Eliade, 1964, p.182). However, the claim that he/she is "indispensable" would appear to be a poor choice of words as, for example, priests undertaking exorcisms have fulfilled this role too, as have others. On the other hand, the shaman's value in such situations is surely not in doubt and can be seen from the results achieved, and in the case of this particular story this is what the youngest son achieves for his father and his sister, with the aid of his servant who acts as his spirit helper.

Eliade then goes on to suggest that the shaman's usefulness in such situations can be attributed to mastery of the techniques of ecstasy:

> [H]is soul can safely abandon his body and roam at vast distances, can penetrate the underworld and rise to the sky. Through his own ecstatic experience he knows the roads of the extraterrestrial regions. He can go below and above because he has already been there. The danger of losing his way in these forbidden regions is still great; but sanctified by his initiation and furnished with his guardian spirits, the shaman is the only human being able to challenge the danger and venture into a mystical geography (Eliade, 1964, p.182).

As has already been mentioned, the shamanic journey frequently involves passing through some kind of gateway, and in this particular story the barrier between the two worlds is represented by a great hole in the ground, which provides access to the Lower World. It is here that the servant not only finds whole rooms full of gold and silver, but also three maidens, "each more beautiful than the other".

After cutting the Divs to pieces and thus demonstrating his superhuman powers, the servant is then hoisted up to the Middle World on a rope by the prince, along with the gold, the silver, and the maidens. On his return home though, the prince finds that in his absence his father had gone blind and his sister mad.

He then learns from his faithful servant that he is in fact a spirit from the Land of the Dead. With the seventy roubles owed to him having been returned and his mission to aid the prince having been accomplished, his time has now come to return there again. Before doing so however, he first tells the prince how to cure his father and sister, and equilibrium is thus restored to the community once more. As for the cure, it involves the prince using the blood of the slaughtered hound to smear his father's eyes with, and a glass of water in which the Div's ears are boiled for his sister to drink.

The exact words of the servant before he goes to his grave indicate that he is gifted with the power of divination: "Smear the blood on your father's eyes; boil the Div's ears in water and give it to your sister to drink; then your father will recover his sight, and your sister her reason. Your father shall vacate the throne for you."

Divination has been defined as "a means of discovering information which cannot be obtained by ordinary means or in an ordinary state of mind" (Vitebsky, 2001, p.104). This would suggest that an astrologer is not in an ordinary state of mind when he constructs a chart and a palmist is not in an ordinary state of mind when he reads the lines on someone's hand. However, there is no reason why this should be the case. Consequently, Harner's definition is to be preferred: "Shamans are especially healers, but they also engage in divination, seeing into the present, past, and future for other members of the community" (Harner, 1990, p.43). To the word "seeing", however, could be added "with the help of the spirits" for as indigenous and neo-shamans alike have pointed out, they do not make use of their own power for this purpose.

The shaman as Diviner may use the method of possession, enter a trance-like state, interpret omens or signs found in events in nature, cast stones, sticks or bones, or he may even look for the patterns in the markings on the liver or the shape of the entrails of an animal. Whatever means he chooses to employ, the underlying belief is always the same – "that the whole universe is interconnected and has a common pattern running through it, so that if the skilled person looks carefully at any one part of it he will be able to read off what is happening in other parts" (Turner, 1971, p.35).

Chapter 5

Georgia & Abkhazia

Despite the fact that Georgia has frequently been invaded by people from outside Europe, including Arabs, Armenians, Turks, Iranians, and Mongols, and despite the fact that the lower-lying southern parts of Georgia would be considered by most people to be part of Asia, when applying for travel insurance Georgia is actually classified as being part of Europe, and the Georgians consider themselves to be Europeans too.

That the Georgians have been able to retain their identity in spite of the incursions referred to above can be attributed in part to the inaccessibility of the mountainous regions of the country, and in part to the unique Georgian language and alphabet. Kartuli, the Georgian language, is part of the Ibero-Caucasian family of languages and is distinct from Indo-European, Turkic, and Semitic languages. It does not have any connection to other Northern Caucasian language groups either, even though it resembles them phonetically. There are in fact two systems of the Georgian alphabet. Khutsuri, which consists of 38 letters and dates back to the fifth century A.D., is used in the Bible and liturgical works. The second Georgian alphabet, Mkherduli, consists of 40 letters and is used in ordinary writing.

Above all, however, the way in which the Georgians have been able to resist being assimilated into alien cultures can probably be attributed to their Orthodox Christian faith, the faith that the people resolutely held on to even when forbidden from openly practicing it in Soviet times. As in other former Soviet states, that faith is now flourishing perhaps as never before. However, the situation was undoubtedly once very different, as we know from the traditional folktales of the people as well as from the pagan rites that are still being performed in the country even today.

> As the hot lamb's blood congealed on her hands, a young woman responded to the questions of a curious visitor. We were standing on the banks of the St'ekura, in the northeast Georgian province of Xevsureti, in the one part of the territory of Xaxmat'i's Jvari not off-limits to females. Not even a hundred kilometres as the crow flies from Tbilisi, we were in a part of Georgia very few Georgians, even now, ever visit; without electricity or all-season roads, it remains an eerily archaic outpost on the remote periphery of Europe. On a chilly July morning, the woman had come to Xevsureti's most sacred shrine, lamb in tow, to undergo the cleansing ritual known as *ganatvla*. She knelt before the priest (*xucesi*) as he intoned a prayer of benediction and healing, invoking St. George, his female partner Samdzimari, and a host of saints, angels and "children of God" (*xvtisšvilni*). He extracted his dagger, and slit the lamb's throat. Its blood spilled forth onto the woman's arms, coating them up to the elbow. Following the ancient principle that the good blood of a slaughtered animal drives out the bad blood of female impurity, she hoped that the sacrifice would free her of certain "impediments" (*dabrk'olebebi*) in her life's course. She saw no contradiction between this ritual and the canons of the Orthodox church; both were integral parts of her Christian faith, both marked her as a Georgian and as a believer (*morc'mune*) (Tuite, 2004, pp.1-2).

According to Charachidzé, the religious system of the northeast Georgian, with its incorporation of Christian symbols and saints in a distinctly non-Christian matrix, "a sombre toute entière voici bientôt trente ans, ne laissant derrière elle que de faibles remous vite disparus" (Charachidzé, 1968, p.717). However, in view of the above description provided by Tuite, this would now appear to be an overly gloomy assessment of the current state of affairs, at least as far as this particular part of the country is concerned. Not surprisingly, it is not a state of affairs that the majority of "civilized" Georgians, aspiring to become future members of NATO and the E.U., are particularly keen on telling the rest of the world about, which is probably one of the reasons why so little field work by outsiders has been done in the region.

Despite the reluctance to accept this aspect of their culture by many Georgians, others have made attempts to identify shamanism in the Caucasus, as Tuite (2004) points out. For example, Nioradze (1940) likened Abkhazian and Georgian "soul-returning" rituals to similar practices performed by Buryat shamans, Bleichsteiner (1936) made ethnographic descriptions from the highland provinces of northeast Georgia available (which were subsequently cited by Eliade in his seminal work on shamanism), and Ochiauri (1954) situated the Xevsur institution of oracles (*kadag*) in Shternberg's evolutionary sequence of stages of divine election, of which Siberian shamanism represents a more primitive manifestation. And as for Charachidzé (1968, 1995), he has defined the Xevsur *kadag* as "chamane", and interprets legendary accounts of past oracles as evidence that until recently the northeast Georgian highlanders had the practice of a "shamanic quest", through which the practitioner received his powers.

Consequently, in the light of all this evidence, the suggestion there is a shamanic tradition in Georgia is not at all far-fetched and it can be found reflected in the folktales from the region.

> [A]lthough Georgia has been a nominally Orthodox Christian country since the 4th century, an indigenous pre-Christian religion was actively practiced in many parts of Georgia up to the beginning of this century and even more recently in some areas, where, with the restriction of official Georgian Orthodox activities under the Soviet regime, syncretistic Christian-pagan rites conducted by the village elders had become the sole forms of worship (Tuite, 1995, p.13).

Even after so many centuries of Christianity in Georgia, many elements of paganism live on in the country to this day:

> Hellenism and Zoroastrianism are long forgotten, but the people have gone back to far older traditions. The cult of the Moon God lives on in the veneration of St George, who is also known as *Tetri Georgi*, or "White George". The Georgian Shrovetide festival of fertility and rebirth is entirely pagan in inspiration. It is called *Berikaoba*, and involves processions and orgiastic carnivals in which the act of sexual intercourse is mimed, and ancient phallic rites are perpetuated from year to year (Burney & Lang, 1971, p.224).

The custom of spending Easter Monday eating and drinking in cemeteries, by the tombs of one's ancestors, clearly has pagan origins too. The Georgian-French scholar Charachidzé describes and analyses Georgian "paganism" in *Le système religieux de la Géorgie païenne* (1968), though it has to be said that not all specialists in the field share his view. The Georgian ethnographer Zurab K'ik'nadze, for example, regards the religious system described by Charachidzé "as an *innovation* cobbled together out of Christian elements in the late middle ages, after Mongol and Persian invasions had cut off the mountains and other peripheral areas from the cultural hegemony of the Orthodox center" (Tuite, 1995, p.13).

Yet another possibility exists, however, which is that the origins of Georgian paganism date back even further into the distant past, when shamanism was practised in the land.

Let us consider Georgian cosmology, for example. As is frequently the case among indigenous peoples who practice shamanism, the universe is believed to consist of three superimposed worlds. They are: "(1) the space above the earth (the celestial world); (2) the earthly space (the surface of the earth); (3) the space below the earth (the netherworld). On the highest level are the gods; on the lowest, the demons and dragons; between the two, in the middle world, men, animals, plants, etc" (Bonnefoy, 1993, p.255).

As for Georgian paganism, it is perhaps best described as a revealed religion, not one that was revealed at the beginning of historical time by means of speech that has been preserved orally or in writing, as is the case with Judaism or Islam, but one that is made manifest each time the soul of a human being is possessed by a *Hat´i* (a divinity). That person, who is then regarded as being officially possessed, becomes a sort of shaman and is known as a *Kadag*. "When the *Kadag* goes into trance, on the occasion of a religious ritual or an event marking individual or collective life, he speaks, and it is then the god who is speaking through his mouth" (Bonnefoy, 1993, p.255). The priest-sacrificer is similarly chosen by what can be termed divine election made manifest through possession. His function however is multi-purpose, not only to perform rites but also to act as the political and military chief of the community.

While the more accessible central lowlands of Georgia have served as a virtual crossroads between the East and the West,

> the inhabitants of the northern Georgian mountain districts, both east and west of the Likhi range — some of which had never yielded to a foreign army until the tsarist period — have held on to their ancient folkways and pre-Christian religious systems to a degree unparalleled in modern Europe. Until very recently, [for example] oracles (kadagebi) practiced their trade within a few dozen kilometers of Tbilisi; [and] animal sacrifices and the pouring of libations, traditions reminiscent of Homeric Greece, are still commonly observed in many parts of Georgia today (Tuite, 1995, p.11).

Additionally, the kind of Georgian spoken in the mountain districts of Pshavi, Khevsureti and parts of Racha, has also limited the influence on the region from outside in that it "bears a stronger resemblance to the literary language of eight centuries ago than to the speech of modern Tbilisi. The Zan dialect spoken in Mingrelia, [for example,] and to an even greater extent the dialects of Svaneti, are incomprehensible to Georgians from other parts of the country" (Tuite, 1995, p.12).

The north Georgian mountain districts in particular thus provide a rich and relatively untapped source of material for both collectors of folklore and anthropologists alike. And in some areas, especially in the provinces of Pshavi, Khevsureti and Tusheti, shrines constructed of stone can be found, many of them adorned with the horns of sacrificed animals, which are still in use today (see Tuite, 1995, p.15).

Although the traditional Georgian religion is commonly described as polytheistic, in fact this is a fallacy as there is a clear distinction between the Supreme God (*Morige Ghmerti*), creator and sustainer of the universe, and all other divine beings, as there is in other so-called polytheistic religions such as Yoruba. And many of the deities have taken on Christian names, as is the case with Santeria in Brazil for example, so that as in some parts of Europe what we find is that the worship of particular saints was actually founded upon the worship of pagan deities.

> Among the principal figures are "St. George" (*Giorgi;* in Svan *Jgëræg*), the "Archangel" (Georgian *Mtavarangelozi;* Svan *Taringzel*), and a hunter deity and protector of wildlife in the high mountains (in Svaneti represented as the goddess *Dæl* or *Dali*). Important female figures include *Barbal* "St. Barbara," a fertility deity and healer of illnesses; and *Lamaria* "St. Mary," protector of women. *Krist'e* "Christ" presides over the world of the dead (Tuite, 1995, p.14).

When we look in more detail into Georgian "paganism", as it has been called, what we find is evidence to indicate that at one point in time some form of shamanism could well have been practised in the region. The people of the northeast, for example, have a Giorgi or Givargi (Saint George) who, like his Svan namesake Jgëræg, watches over men and protects them on those occasions when they leave the village to seek the riches of the outside world. And like Jgëræg, he has a female counterpart: known as Samdzimari or Samdzivari:

> In a myth transmitted through Xevsurian epic poetry, Giorgi and his human scout, a legendary oracle named Gaxua who underwent temporary death in order to make the trip, descended into the hypochthonian kingdom of the Kajes ... a race of supernatural blacksmiths with magical powers. There Giorgi succeeds in annihilating the Kaj army, whereupon he takes possession of their metalworking equipment, their treasures, a one-horned cow, and three daughters of the king of the Kajes, one of whom is Samdzimari [also known as Samdzivari] (Tuite, 2006, p.169).

As well as the Saint George of the mountains, there is also the Saint George of the Georgian plains, the only divinity whose worship has been more or less preserved in Plains Georgia. Possession plays an important part in his rituals, but unlike in the mountains, the possessed are generally women, whose souls are seized to punish them for sins they are said to have committed (see Bonnefoy, 1993, p.257).

This descent into the kingdom of Kajes can be described as a shamanic journey of initiation from which Giorgi brings back a spirit helper. Evidence to support this hypothesis is the fact that Samdzimari, like Dæl in Svaneti, can be described as "the mediatrix par excellence, in the context of a religious system in which women, human or supernatural, frequently appear in this role: legendary male oracles (Geo. *kadag*) are said to receive their communicative powers through the experience of nightly visits from Samdzimari, who can take on the form of a mortal woman" Tuite, 2006, p.169). Her main function is to intervene "between the shaman and his god when the contact is broken. Always available, she takes possession of the abandoned shaman's soul and reestablishes the link with the departed god" (Bonnefoy, 1993, pp.259-260). Thus one of Samdzimari's key attributes is her ability to circulate between inaccessible spaces and human society – in other words, to act as an intermediary or mediator between people and divine beings, which is very much the role a shaman plays.

There is also evidence to indicate that there were psychopomps, another role traditionally undertaken by shamans. Contact with the souls of the dead, for example, is entrusted to the female mesultane ("she who is with the souls"), whereas the male kadag (oracle) requires the services of Samdzimari to do so. There were also mgebari (escorts) who took on the role of accompanying the newly deceased to the "Land of Souls", more commonly known in shamanic cosmologies as the Land of the Dead. The word psychopomp, etymologically, means "a deliverer of souls" and is derived from two Ancient Greek words – psyche meaning "soul" or "spirit," and pompos meaning "sending." Other examples of figures who have acted as psychopomps include Ganesh the doorkeeper in Hindu mythology, Hermes, Mercury, the Greek Ferryman of the River Styx, the Christian Holy Spirit, and the Norse Heimdal. The Greeks and Romans believed the dead were ferried across the river Styx by a boatman named Charon, and they paid him by placing a coin in the mouth of the deceased.

The Land of the Dead played a significant part in the belief system of the Ancient Egyptians too, as can be seen from the texts of the so called Egyptian Book of the Dead, the *Pert em hru,* which reveal the unalterable belief of the Egyptians in the immortality of the soul, resurrection, and life after death. The sacred temple mysteries of Isis and Osiris gave initiates the opportunity to come to terms with death long before old age or disease made it obligatory to do so, and to conquer it by discovering their own immortality (see Grof, 1994, pp.9-11).

> ... Until as late as the 1950's in some localities, women of the northeast Georgian highlands gave birth in crudely-built huts (*sachexi* or *k'oxi*), located at some distance outside the village. The new mother and her child were considered extremely "impure" during the first weeks after birth, and were only gradually (re)integrated into the community through a series of purifications, sacrifices and the child's formal presentation at the clan sanctuary (xat'shi mibareba) [Mindadze & Didebulidze 1997] (Tuite, 2006, p.176).

This marked the child's definitive transfer from the lineage of the mother to the father's clan and the newly dead followed the same pathway, being escorted by their mgebari to the equivalent of a clan in the "Land of Souls", known as Suleti.

For further evidence to support the hypothesis that some form of shamanism was once practised in the region, we can point to the images of Dæl in Svan oral literature and ritual, in which she takes on the form of a shape-shifter, an attribute again commonly associated with shamans, in the story of Dæl and the doomed hunter, for example:

> The story starts off with an encounter between the goddess and a legendary hunter called Betgil, selected by Dæl to be her lover. She gives him a token of their love in the form of a bead, ring or charm (depending on the version of the story) and then makes him promise to avoid all contact with human females from that day on, even including his own wife. For as long as he remains in the goddess's good graces Betgil enjoys remarkable success in the hunt. When one day, however, he breaks his promise, sleeping with either his wife or his sister-in-law, the goddess changes herself into a white chamois and chases after him as he tries to escape by climbing up a mountain. On reaching the

> summit the goddess resumes her original form and confronts the terrified Betgil, who falls (or some say jumps) to his death on the rocks below (see Tuite, 2006, p.166).

Xevsur shrines that are consecrated to Samdzimari by name, or other female spirits with similar characteristics, are known to every Pshav and Xevsur community. And associated with the male-gendered patron deities (called *xvtisshvilni* "children of God") of villages are auxiliary goddesses, not only capable of assuring the health and fertility of people and their livestock but also with the potential of bringing harm, thus reflecting what is generally found to be the case in shamanism – the eristic nature of the spirits (see Tuite, 2006, p.170).

What we have seen is that both Dæl and Samdzimari, by either crossing out of or into relatively stable or fixed structures, or by operating "betwixt and between" the margins of these structures, are endowed with the ability to operate within liminal states in the same way that shamans traditionally do for the purpose of mediating between the two worlds (see Tuite, 2006, pp.181-182). Not only that, but it is also interesting to note that encounters between the goddesses and their mortal lovers characteristically take place in liminal locations too: "mountains or pastures, at the frontier between the spatial domain of the human community ('culture') and the inaccessible spaces appertaining to nature, the dwelling places of gods and spirits" (Tuite, 2006, p.182). All this points to the very strong likelihood that some form of shamanism was practised in the region, and this is reflected in the folktales of the country.

> [E]ven before the Soviets this was a land of myths and tales as tall as the peaks themselves … In Armenia, Noah's Ark lies on the borders. In Azerbaijan, the Garden of Eden is said to lurk somewhere in the south. Georgia is not to be outdone. If her neighbours boast of the genesis of man, Georgia claims to have

> been home to the gods. Prometheus was bound to one of her great peaks, his liver torn daily by the circling birds of prey (Griffin, 2001, p.2).

Not only are Georgians reputed to be descendants of Thargamos, the great-grandson of Japhet, son of the Biblical Noah (and Thargamos is the Torgom of Armenian tradition), but the ancient name of Georgia was Colchis, which was associated for centuries with the Greek myth of Jason and his fifty Argonauts, who sailed from Greece to Colchis to capture the Golden Fleece. It should therefore come as no surprise that Georgia contains a rich source of traditional tales, or that the stories are the products of so many different influences – including pagan, Christian and Islamic – in view of the troubled history of the land.

In shamanism the notion of interdependence "is the idea of the kinship of all life, the recognition that nothing can exist in and of itself without being in relationship to other things, and therefore that it is insane for us to consider ourselves as essentially unrelated parts of the whole Earth" (Halifax in Nicholson, (comp.), 1987, p.220). And through neurotheology, this assertion so often heard expressed in neo-shamanic circles that all life is connected, can now be substantiated:

> Through the new medical discipline of neurotheology developed largely at the Massachusetts Institute of Technology, it has been shown that during mystical ecstasy (or its equivalent, entheogenic shamanic states [states induced by ingesting hallucinogens]), the individual experiences a blurring of the boundaries on the ego and feels at "one with Nature"; the ego is no longer confined within the body, but extends outward to all of Nature; other living beings come to share in the ego, as an authentic communion with the total environment, which is sensed as in some way divine (Ruck, Staples, et al., 2007, p.76).

The peculiar interconnectedness of communities through ties of family and obligation found in Georgian society would suggest that this is a concept that Georgians are more than familiar with. Rather than being a product of Soviet rule, the sharing or pooling resources and wealth has long been practised by the people. It has also served to sustain them through the recent hardships they have had to endure.

Although the form of social organization practised can best be described as patriarchal, with all authority being vested in the head of the family group – the *mamasakhlisi,* literally "the father of the house", it is likely that it was originally matriarchal. For when hunting was the basis of the economic life of the community, when the men were frequently absent on expeditions in search of food and the mortality rate among them was high, the women would have acted as heads of the households. And this continued among the mountain peoples until relatively recently (see Allen, 1932, p.35).

Another reason to believe that the organization of society was once matriarchal can be found in the language. One of the features that makes the Georgian language unique in that it has the odd distinction of reversing the almost universal sounds for mother and father, so that *mama* is father and *deda* is mother, which could well indicate that the tribal peoples who inhabited the region were at one point in time matriarchal, worshipping the sun, not the moon, as the supreme female deity and that they passed on their lines of descent through the mothers' rather than through the fathers' side. And even today, though the Georgian language has no genders, the sun, *mze,* is still thought of as feminine (see Anderson, 2003, p.151). Although there is no mention of hereditary shamans as such in the history of Georgian paganism, the *khevisberi* in the northeast Georgian highlands would seem to have fulfilled a similar role. It was

the *khevisberi,* far more than any distant priest or power, who

> directed the spiritual, ritual and moral affairs of the mountains. He was and is elected by his peers, not on the basis of age or wealth, but for his deeper qualities [specialized ritual, mythological, and esoteric knowledge inherited from his ancestors]. Sometimes his office is given to him in dreams. He decides on all questions of law, presides over festivals and sacred ceremonies; he, alone, approaches the shrine and undertakes the sacrifice and in so doing brings peace to the dead and placates the deities (Anderson, 2003, p.144).

As for the shrine, the sacred space where ceremonies are performed, it is known as the *khati.* It is the place

> where people gather to make offerings, to eat and drink and sacrifice and also to dance and sing ritual, improvised songs, the *kaphiaoba*. The word *khati* has other significant religious and spiritual meanings [too]: it is the name given to the Sons of God, pre-Christian deities like *gudani* and *lashari,* to whom the mountain people gave special devotion, and it also means "icon" or just "image" (Anderson, 2003, p.97).

What we can see from this is that shamanism, albeit it under different names and in various forms, has thrived for millennia and, it has to be said that it is hard to imagine a tradition surviving for so long in so many cultures unless there were effective components to it (see Walsh, 2007, pp.120).

No introduction to Georgia would be complete without saying a few words about the hospitality of the people.

> Hospitality and generosity towards a guest are still, and always have been, paramount. A guest can do no wrong. There are stories of a guest violating the host's wife, without receiving a complaint while he is still a guest; but of the host accompanying his guest to the borders of his territory, and then killing him as

soon as he steps across the boundary (Dolidze, 1999, p.7).

As anyone visiting Georgia will find, however poor people may be, they always make an effort to hide this from their guests and to lay on suppers that are legendary.

> Part of the ritual of hospitality is the meal: dinner or supper. Generally these will be elaborate affairs lasting several hours, with family and friends sitting at a large table, covered with all manner of dishes. During the dinner, many toasts will be proposed, in speeches often lasting for several minutes or more, and large quantities of wine will be drunk. This part of the ritual is conducted by men, who need a good capacity for alcohol. The women will generally eat a normal meal, with a glass or two of wine, but with no obligation to drink more (Dolidze, 1999, p.7).

And this is how the Canadian anthropologist and researcher Kevin Tuite describes the suppers:

> The Georgian *supra* ...can go on all evening into the wee hours of the morning, with each guest consuming several litres of wine. These heroic quantities of alcohol are drunk in accordance with strict rules: the participant in a *supra* must pronounce a toast — to another guest, to Georgia, to the souls of the departed, etc. — before drinking each glass, or drinking horn, of wine. The toasts are frequently occasions for a display of eloquence, and are accompanied by song and recitations of poetry (Tuite, 1995, p.13).

Although to us the lavishness of such entertaining may well appear to be "over the top", it certainly does not seem so to the Georgians who host these banquets. For "In these celebrations of life and of their bonds to each other, they have discovered a uniquely effective way of making life bearable under the most adverse circumstances" (Tuite, 1995, p.13). We need to bear in mind that up until only recently life was nothing but grim for most of the people and this would have been one of the few ways available to them of escaping from it all.

The Tale of the Hunter and the Giant Eagle

It happened and yet nothing happened – there lived a poor hunter. So one day he was hunting and he sees, lying there, sprawled over three oak trees, is an eagle. The hunter took aim with his bow, but the eagle says, "Do not kill me, I am still a nestling. Take me home, and nurse me; I have a broken wing. I will be of use to you".

The hunter did not kill the eagle. He took him home, and he began to nurse him. But his wife is angry: "There is nothing for us to eat, yet you drag home an eagle". He treated him for two weeks, the hunter cured the eagle. The eagle said, "Now take me out to those oak trees".

The hunter took him out. The eagle flew up, tore out one oak and threw it beyond three mountains. "No, I am not yet cured", said the eagle. "Let us go, and nurse me some more". Again the hunter brought the eagle home.

His wife is angry: "For ourselves there is nothing, but yet you have brought him again!"

For two more weeks the hunter treated the eagle. "Take me to those oaks", said the eagle.

The hunter took him out to them. The eagle flew up, seized the second oak, tore it out, and threw it beyond nine mountains. "I am still not healed. Take me home again and nurse me", says the eagle. Once again the hunter took the eagle home. Again his wife is angry, but the hunter does not listen. He treats the eagle and feeds him. He nursed him for two more weeks. "All right, now take me!" said the eagle.

The hunter took him there. The eagle took off. He flew, pulled out the third oak, and threw it; and nobody could tell where it went to. The eagle said, "Now I am cured. Slaughter an ox, bring it with you, sit yourself on me and we will fly to my father and mother. They will pour out in front of you all their wealth, but do not take anything. Ask them to give you only the rusty old casket which they have".

The hunter went and slaughtered an ox. He himself climbed upon the eagle and put the ox on it too. The eagle took off and flew, and takes him up higher and higher. The eagle turns his head to the hunter, the hunter cuts off a piece of meat from the ox and puts it in the eagle's beak. They had all but arrived, when the eagle turned his head, but the ox is all finished. The hunter cut off a piece of meat from himself under his knee and gave it to the eagle. "This is tasty, such tasty meat!" says the eagle. They flew in. The hunter got off, he is limping. "Why are you limping?" asks the eagle.

"That meat which you praised, that was my flesh; the ox itself was all finished". The eagle passed his wing along the hunter's leg, and the leg was made whole.

The eagle brought the hunter to his mother and says, "Mother, I was lying with a broken wing, and this man saved me from death. Reward him, give him whatever he asks for".

The eagle's mother poured out in front of the hunter gold, silver, pearls, semi-precious stones, cloths and caps, but the hunter does not take anything. "Which do you want?" asked the eagle's mother.

"Give me your rusty casket".

The eagle's mother got still more jewels, still better and more beautiful, but the hunter does not take anything; he has got up and he is walking away. "All right, go and take what you want", said the eagle's mother. The hunter turned round, and the eagle's mother displayed in front of him still more wealth. The hunter did not even look at it. He got up and is altogether on the point of going away. "Go and help yourself", says the eagle's mother, but she does not give him the casket, she only shows him various riches. The hunter does not even take anything in his hands, he simply walks away. The eagle's mother brought him back a third time and gave him the casket. She said, "Beware, do not touch the casket. Do not open it until you reach home, otherwise you will be sorry".

The eagle sat the hunter on his back, flew down, let him alight and flew away. The hunter is walking. He is carrying the casket, and thinking, "But suppose they have cheated me and palmed off an empty casket on me. Why don't I have a look and see what is lying there. Perhaps there is something there that will kill me". He opened the casket, and there came out from it shops, houses, palaces: a huge town spread itself out. Merchants are running about the town, making a fuss, making a noise. Trading is going on, and life is in full swing. But the hunter stands and looks. He does not know how to drive all this back into the casket and close it up. He is standing racking his brains, and tearing his hair.

At this time a *dev* comes. "What are you upset about, man?"

"And why wouldn't one be upset? I opened the casket, and a whole town grew out of it. But how to put it all back and close the casket, I do not know".

"And what will you give for my help?" says the *dev*. "Will you give me something which you do not know about?"

"I will give it", said the hunter. "Why not?" The hunter did not know that his wife had given birth to a golden-curled son while he was flying with the eagle.

The *dev* closed the casket and drove the whole town inside it, just as it had been, so there was only the bare field left. "In my own time I will ask for what was promised, and you will send it", said the *dev*.

The hunter came home, and he opened the casket. There came out shops, houses, palaces; there grew up a huge town. Merchants are walking through the town. They are trading, making a fuss, making a noise. The hunter became the master of the whole town. Only the fate of his son grieves him: the *dev* requires what has been promised. And he will not give up.

The time came, and this golden-curled young man got up and went to the *dev.* He walked, he walked, and he met an old woman. "Where are you going, little son?" asks the old woman.

"To the *dev*, as food", he says.

"Little son", said the old woman, "pass though this way, and you will see a river. The *dev's* daughters come to that river to bathe. Hide yourself there. The one who is tallest, that is the eldest, the shorter one, that is the middle one, but the shortest of all, she is the youngest; steal her clothes and hide them. The sisters will go away, but she will remain undressed. Whatever she does do not give her her clothes, and she will become your wife. In everything she will help you and deliver you from your misfortune".

The young man performed everything exactly as the old woman had taught him. He went to that river, hid himself and lay in wait for the sisters. The sisters came, they undressed, and are bathing. The young man came out, took the clothes of the youngest one and hid them. The sisters finished bathing, and came out of the water. The older ones dressed and went away, but the youngest one remained alone. She looked for her clothes, but she did not find them and she called, "Who are you? Come out, show yourself. You be my brother, and I will be your sister!" The young man does not come out. Once more the girl called, "Come out, show yourself, you be my brother, and I will be your sister!" The young man does not come out. Then the girl called, "Come out, show yourself, let it be as you wish: you be my husband and I will be your wife!"

He came out and he gave her clothes. The girl glanced at him, and the golden-curled young man pleased her. She asked, "Who are you and what brought you here?"

"I am going as food to your father".

"Do not be afraid", she said, "just tell me when things

become difficult".

The young man went to the *dev.* The *dev* said, "I will order you to do one thing. If you do not fulfil it, then know that I will eat you. In a single night cover the whole house and yard with gold cloth".

The young man went sadly to his wife. "Such and such your father orders. What is there to do?"

"You go to sleep", said his wife, "I will do it all myself". She called together her people and ordered them to cover with gold cloth all the yard and the house. In the morning she said to her husband, "Go and sit there, touching it up here and there, as if you had woven it all". The *dev* came out, and looks. The young man is sitting and touching up the gold cloths.

What could the *dev* do? He ordered the young man, "Erect for me by the morning such a palace that even the king would not be ashamed to enter that palace".

The young man went to his wife and she said, "You go to sleep, I myself will organise everything". He lay down and went to sleep. His wife called her people and said, "Well now, work adroitly, on you is our only hope!" By the morning they built a palace; if you look at it you cannot take your eyes away.

In the morning the wife said to her husband. "Get up, climb on top, take a hammer and knock a little, as if something was unfinished during the night". The young man climbed up, holding a hammer and tapping. The *dev* came out, and sees a wonderful castle standing. He bit his lip but what could he do?

The *dev* said, "I have an unbroken horse; if you break him in, good, but if not, then I will eat you".

"All right", said the young man. He went to his wife and told her, "Your father has an unbroken horse, it is necessary to break him in".

"Everything before was nothing", said his wife, "the real business is only now beginning. My father himself becomes the horse, but you have to break him in. I will give you the bit, and you put it on him. And besides that, take with you a small iron hammer: when he flies up, hit him on the head, and when he goes down bang him on the nose. Do not look at him with pity, but hit him with all your strength, otherwise you will not get away alive".

In the morning the young man took the bit and the iron hammer. He went and sat on the horse, and the horse flew up to the sky. As the horse is flying upwards, the young man hits him on the head with the iron hammer; he hits him with all his strength. And as the horse dives down, he smashes him on the nose. He beat him up unmercifully. The horse got tired. He was worn out, he hardly stayed alive. The young man led the horse away to the stable, took of the bit and walked away.

The horse turned back into a *dev* and stood in the doorway. "Well, then, did you break in the horse?" he asks.

The young man looks, and the *dev's* muzzle is all bloody. "What is wrong with you?" he asks.

"It was you who served me like this", says the *dev*, "the horse on which you were sitting was me. But tomorrow I am going to eat you all the same, you will not be saved".

The young man was frightened and he goes to his wife: "Well then, did you break in the horse?" his wife asks.

"Tomorrow your father will eat me all the same", said her husband.

That night the husband and wife got up and went. They walk, and they run, as much as their strength allows. When it became light the *dev* found out that they had run away and he chased after them. The husband and wife are running. "Look back, is anybody pursuing?" said the wife.

The husband looked back. "Something in the distance the size of a fly can be seen". The wife turned herself into a cornfield, the husband into a reaper. The reaper stands, he is dripping with sweat.

The *dev* approached and asked, "Did not a young man and a

girl pass by here?"

"The whole day I reap, and after that I leave. What are passers to me?" says the reaper. "I have not seen anybody". The *dev* returned home. The cornfield once again became a girl and the reaper the young man, and they went further.

The *dev* came home, he says to his wife, "I did not find anybody!"

"Was there absolutely nobody?" asked the wife.

"Absolutely not: in one place there stood a wheatfield and a reaper was reaping it. I approached him and asked him, but he had not seen anybody".

"But that was really your daughter and your son-in-law", says the *dev's* wife. The *dev* chased after the fugitives.

The wife says to her husband, "Look around, can anybody be seen?"

"Something the size of a fly can be seen", says her husband.

"That is my father". The girl became a dense forest, and the rays of the sun do not penetrate into her virgin breast, and the young man becomes an old man; the old man wanders near the forest and picks up sticks.

The *dev* approached. "A young man and a girl did not pass here?"

"I swear that, to this forest, ever since it has stood here, not a single person except you, has come. I am an old man, why should I bother about people passing?" The *dev* turned round and went home. Then forest became the girl, and the old man, the young man, and they went on their way.

But the *dev* comes home. "What, didn't you catch up with them, didn't you take them?" asks the *dev's* wife.

"No", said the *dev,* "I found nobody who might have seen them. On the road I only met with one old man. He was picking up sticks by the forest, but besides that there was nobody".

"Ach, you are a fool! That forest was your daughter, and that old man was your son-in-law. Now I myself will set out, and we will see how they will get away from us". They sat on their horses and rode in pursuit.

The fugitives are hurrying, the *dev* and his wife are catching up with them. The girl said, "Look around, is there anybody chasing us?"

The young man looked round, and he says, "Something the size of a fly can be seen".

"That is my father", said the daughter. She looked, and she sees there are two of them. "And mother is with him, now indeed we cannot be saved". She became a bottomless lake, and he a duck.

The *dev* and his wife approach and see a shining lake, and a duck swimming on the lake. The *dev's* wife went close up to the lake, and she drinks. She wants to dry out the whole lake. The *dev* also drinks. They drank and they drank and they burst.

The lake became the girl, and the duck, the young man. They embraced each other and kissed each other for joy. They sat on the *dev's* horses and rode to that young man's father. ("Zgapari monadirisa da didi artsivisa". Recorded by T.Razikashvili, in the village of Kheltubani. Published in the collection "Folk tales collected in Kartli by Tedo Razikashvili", Tiflis, 1909. Taken from Dolidze, N.I. (1999) *Georgian Folk Tales,* Tbilisi: Merani Publishing House).

***

Traditionally told tales often start with a few words at the beginning that are designed to get listeners ready for a different kind of discourse: a long narrative that we do not suppose to be literally true, set in a kind of dreamtime that is apart from, but closely involved with, ordinary reality. The standard opener we all know is, "Once upon a time." However, one of the standard openers commonly found in Georgian folktales is the one this particular story starts with: "It happened and yet nothing happened".

This is how the standard introduction is explained in the story *The Tale of Tales,* which comes from *Yes and No Stories: A Book of Georgian Folk Tales* written by George Papashvily, an author who immigrated to the United States from Georgia in the 1920s: "[S]tories always begin the same way–There was, there was, and yet there was not–. It means that what comes after is true and true but then again not so true. Or perhaps it means that what is true for two men is not true for three."

What we have in this formulaic introduction is also an example of what has been referred to as "the alteration or the transmutation of space" (Eliade, 1981, p.10). As was pointed out in the opening chapter, this is a theme that appears over and over again in shamanic stories, wherever they happen to come from.

One of the first features one notices about *The Tale of the Hunter and the Giant Eagle* is that the focus is mainly on the action. The observation is made in the Introduction to *Georgian Folk Tales* that "Whilst a written, 'literary' novel or short story might devote paragraphs to descriptions of people or places, these tales usually settle for an adjective or two" (Hunt, 1999, p.8). This would seem to be a feature of shamanic stories in general and can also be found in other examples of the genre.

As for the journey undertaken by the hunter in the tale, a journey takes place in a landscape – real or imaginary, in this world or in the world of non-ordinary reality. Although the cosmology through which the shamanic journey takes place will vary from culture to culture, the structure of the whole cosmos is frequently symbolized by the number seven, which is made up of the four directions, the centre, the zenith in heaven, and the nadir in the underworld. The essential axes of this structure are the four cardinal points and a central vertical axis passing through their point of intersection that connects the Upper World, the Middle World and the Lower World. The names by which the central vertical axis that connects the three worlds is referred to include the world pole, the tree of life, the sacred mountain, the central house pole, and Jacob's ladder; and so important is this cosmology considered to be that religion itself has been described by Berger (1969) as the enterprise we undertake to establish just such a sacred cosmos.

Different types of shamanic journeys can be undertaken – to the Lower World, to the Middle World, or to the Upper World. Journeys are also undertaken to the Land of the Dead, where the shaman acts as a psychopomp – a conductor of souls – and sometimes the Land of the Dead is antipodal, meaning everything there is reversed: day here is night there, and vice versa. There are also journeys for the purpose of divination and journeys to carry out soul retrievals.

How can these other worlds be accessed? The journey frequently involves passing through some kind of gateway. As Eliade explains,

> The "clashing of rocks," the "dancing reeds," the gates in the shape of jaws, the "two razor-edged restless mountains," the "two clashing icebergs," the "active door," the "revolving barrier," the door made of the two halves of the eagle's beak, and many more – all these are images used in myths and sagas to suggest the insurmountable difficulties of passage to the Other World (Eliade, 2003, pp.64-65).

And to make such a journey requires a change in one's mode of being, entering a transcendent state, which makes it possible to attain the world of spirit. In *The Tale of the Hunter and the Giant Eagle,* as we have seen, the hunter is required to be partly consumed in order to access the Upper World where he can find the help he is after.

In a number of cultures the initiation of a shaman involves dismemberment and/or consumption by the spirits. In some cases, as among the Yakut, the candidate's dismembered pieces are distributed among disease spirits as an offering to give the shaman power over those diseases. Likewise, to enter into contracts with spirits or to obtain guardians, a candidate of the Plains tribes will offer the spirits (in animal forms) his own flesh to eat. These can be seen as metaphors for the death and utter discorporation of the old self, or else as the candidate's own ecstatic visions. As for the reconstitution of the initiate, this nearly always involves the building of a new spiritual body, whether through being consumed and regurgitated by spirits, being stirred in a boiling pot and pieced back together, having the brains washed and/or replaced, or having bones replaced by magical materials such as quartz crystal or diamond. In *The Tale of the Hunter and the Giant Eagle* the process of initiation is represented by the hunter cutting a piece of meat from himself, under his knee, and giving it to the eagle to eat. The eagle then passes his wing along the hunter's leg, and the leg is made whole again.

> Ascent and flight are proofs par excellence of the divinization of man. The specialists in the sacred – medicine men, shamans, mystics – are above all men who are believed to fly up to Heaven, in ecstasy or even in the flesh ... The descent to the Underworld and the ascent to Heaven obviously denote different religious experiences; but the two experiences spectacularly prove that he who has undergone them has transcended the secular condition of humanity and that his behaviour is purely that of a spirit (Eliade, 2003, p.78).

In *The Tale of the Hunter and the Giant Eagle,* it is the eagle that provides the hunter with the means of accessing the Upper World. However, there are of course many other ways of getting there too:

> [S]tairs are only one of the numerous symbolic expressions for ascent [cf.the story of Jacob's Ladder from the Old Testament for an example of this]; the sky can be reached by fire or smoke, by

> climbing a tree or a mountain, or ascending by way of a rope, or vine, the rainbow, or even a sunbeam, for example. Finally, we must mention another group of myths and legends related to the theme of ascent – the "chain of arrows." … A volume would be required for an adequate exposition of these mythical motifs and their ritual implications (Eliade, 1964, pp.490-491).

It has been proposed that "the mystical experience, in whatever religion it may be cradled, always implies a celestial ascension" (Eliade, 1991, p.166). However, within cultures where shamanism is practised, mystical experiences are also possible through journeys to what are known as the Lower World and the Middle World. Indeed, it is a Middle World journey that is undertaken by the hunter's son in *The Tale of the Hunter and the Giant Eagle*. Journeys to the Land of the Dead, where mystical experiences can take place, are possible too. Eliade's hypothesis, based on the Judeo-Christian concept of Heaven and Hell, would thus seem to be flawed.

> It has been observed that no one can engage in a religious ceremony of any importance without submitting to a kind of preparatory initiation that introduces him gradually into the sacred world. This can take the form of anointings, purifications, and blessings – all essentially positive operations. But the same result can be achieved through fasts, vigils, retreat, and silence, that is by ritual abstinences that are nothing more than the practical application of specific prohibitions (Durkheim, 2001, p.230).

In other words, ascetic practices can be a means of setting the scene prior to entering sacred space, the first of the three stages of ceremony. To abstain from something that is useful or that answers to some human need clearly entails discomfort, and this becomes asceticism proper when practised as a way of life. Normally the negative cult serves only as a form of preparation for the positive cult, and an example of this would be the rites of puberty or the initiatory rites that the apprentice shaman has to undergo. In *The Tale of the Hunter and the Giant Eagle,* it takes the form of the hunter feeding his own flesh to the eagle. And it is of course not only the goals pursued by apprentice shamans that call for ascetic practices to bring about transmutation – the same is required of other mystics too, such as yogis.

According to James, asceticism symbolizes "the belief that there is an element of real wrongness in this world, which is neither to be ignored nor evaded, but which must be squarely met and overcome by an appeal to the soul's heroic resources, and neutralized and cleansed away by suffering" (James, 1982, p.362). However, for initiates it has no such symbolism. It is merely their apprenticeship, part of a necessary process before they can become accepted by both their teachers and the people they will ultimately represent.

Ordeals the apprentice might be required to undergo in non-ordinary reality during his/her initiation could include torture and violent dismemberment of the body, the scraping away of the flesh until the body is reduced to a skeleton, the substitution of viscera and renewal of the blood, and even a period spent in Hell during which the future shaman is taught by the souls of dead shamans and by demons (see Eliade, 2003, p.96).

Again and again in stories "we see how things appear in threes: how things have to happen three times, how the hero is given three wishes; how Cinderella goes to the ball three times; how the hero or the heroine is the third of three children" (Booker, 2004, p.229). In *The Tale of the Hunter and the Giant Eagle,* the eagle requires three periods of nursing, the hunter's son is set three challenges by the *dev,* and the hunter's son and the *dev's* daughter are required to shape-shift three times in order to escape.

Not only does the number three appear in many folktales, (three brothers or sisters, three tasks to accomplish, three encounters, three guesses, three little pigs, three bears), but it also has mystical and spiritual associations. In ancient Babylon the three primary gods were Anu, Bel (Baal), and Ea, representing Heaven, Earth, and the Abyss. Similarly, there were three aspects to the Egyptian sun god: Khepri (rising), Re (midday), and Atum (setting). And in Christianity there is the Trinity of God the Father, God the Son, and God the Holy Spirit.

Shape-shifters, like the *dev's* youngest daughter, are beings who have the ability to transform themselves (mentally or physically) into animals. A "theriomorph" is a shape-shifter; a being who can assume an animal as well as a human form. There are two types of shape-shifting; changing your light body in the astral to power animal, and changing your physical form on the earth plane into an animal. In myths and ancient pictographs, the shaman is often characterized by the distinctive ability to change himself from human into animal shape. Sometimes this change is a literal one, human flesh transformed into animal flesh or covered over by animal skin; in other accounts, the soul leaves the shaman's unconscious body to enter into the body of an animal, fish or bird.

It is not only shamans who have such powers according to tales from around the globe. Shape-shifting is part of a mythic and storytelling tradition stretching back over thousands of years. The gods of various mythologies are credited with this ability, as are the heroes of the great epic sagas.

In Nordic myth, Odin could change his shape into any beast or bird; in Greek myth, Zeus often assumed animal shape in his relentless pursuit of young women. Cernunnos, the lord of animals in Celtic mythology, wore the shape of a stag, and also the shape of a man with a heavy rack of horns. In the *Odyssey*, Homer tells the tale of Proteus – a famous soothsayer who would not give away his knowledge unless forced to do so. Menelaus came upon him while he slept, and held on to him tightly as he shape-shifted into a lion, a snake, a leopard, a bear, etc. Defeated, Proteus returned to his own shape and Menelaus won the answers to his questions.

Shape-shifters can also be found in fairy tales. The transformed husband, wife or lover is a common theme. "Beauty and the Beast", from 18th-century France, is probably the best known of the many "animal bridegroom" stories to be found around the world.

Not all transformations are from human to animal shape. *The Great Selkie of Sule Skerry*, described in Scottish legends and ballads, is "a man upon dry land, a selkie [seal] in the sea," and he leaves a human maid pregnant with his child. Irish legends tell of men who marry seal or otter women, hiding their animal skins from them so that they cannot return to the water. Generally these women bear several sons, but pine away for their true home. If they manage to find the skin, they then return to the sea with barely a thought for the ones left behind.

Japanese fairy tales warn of the danger of *kitsune*, the fox-wife. The fox takes on the form of a beautiful woman in these stories, but to wed her brings madness and death. In Tibet, a frog-husband is an unexpected source of joy to a shy young bride. He is not a man disguised as a frog but a frog disguised as a man. When his young wife burns his frog skin to keep her lover in the shape she prefers, the frog-husband loses his magical powers, gracefully resigning himself to ordinary human life instead. In Native American legends, deer maidens are dangerous. In a Lakota version of the tale, a young man walking far from camp meets a beautiful woman alone in the woods. It is (he thinks) the very woman he has been courting, who has rejected him. On this occasion, however, she seems to be interested in him and looks even more beautiful than ever in her doeskin robe. While they talk, he playfully threads the end of a rope through a hole in her robe–until a dog appears and barks at her. The young woman panics and turns to flee, returning to her own deer-shape, but the rope holds the deer maiden fast around her foreleg. "Let me go!" she cries. "If you let me go, I'll give you magical power." The man releases her warily, and the deer maiden disappears through the wood. He vomits profusely, sick with the knowledge that if he had made love to her he would have gone mad like other young men who had encountered the deer.

After this, he lives alone, plagued by sudden fits of wild, deer-like behavior. Yet the deer-woman keeps her promise and gives him this ability: his skill with horses is unsurpassed and also with other four-legged creatures. Stories of shape-shifters let us journey into non-ordinary reality, at least in our imaginations, and they enable us to inhabit many skins. Above all, they serve to remind us that we are all living beings beneath the fur, the feathers, and the scales.

Shape-shifting can be viewed as the imitation of the actions and voices of animals, though the shaman himself would certainly not describe what he does in such terms. During his apprenticeship, the future shaman has to learn the secret language required to communicate with the animal spirits and how to take possession of them, and this is often the "animal language" itself or a form of language derived from animal cries. It is regarded as equivalent to knowing the secrets of nature and hence evidence of the ability to be able to prophesy. And by sharing in the animal mode of being, the shaman can be seen to be re-establishing the situation that existed in mythical times, when man and animal were one (see Eliade, 1989, pp.96-98).

The first instance of shape-shifting in the tale presented here occurs when the hunter's son steals the clothes of the *dev's* youngest daughter. This transforms the youngest daughter into her human form, thus enabling him to establish a relationship with her.

"The human-horse relationship is clearly an important one 'in a region with extensive uninhabited areas, in which one's horse may have literally meant the difference between life and death" (Dolidze, 1999, p.9), and the connection felt between mountaineer and horse in Georgia is probably as ancient as their myths. There is, for example, a Georgian legend that asks, "Who were my ancestors?" And the answer given is "He who pulled milk out of a wild mare's udder with his lips and grew drunk as a little foal" Consequently, the fact that it is a horse that the *dev* transforms himself into would come as no surprise to anyone familiar with both the geography and history of the land.

In her role as an intermediary, "the shaman can be seen to be responsible for maintaining the balance of the community and for creating the harmony from which life springs" (Halifax, 1991, p.15). In *The Tale of the Hunter and the Giant Eagle* this is achieved by the *dev's* daughter ensuring the survival of the hunter's son and then ridding the community of her evil parents.

As intermediary, the shaman can be said to serve as a bridge or a link – "to facilitate the changing of condition without violent social disruptions or an abrupt cessation of individual and collective life" (Van Gennep, 1977, p.48). Being regarded as an outsider gives the shaman an advantage as it enables him/her to "to criticize all structure-bound personae in terms of a moral order binding on all, and also to mediate between all segments or components of the structured system" (Turner, 1995, p.116-117).

When I spoke to Rusudan Choloq'ashvili (author of the 2004 publication *Imagery and Beliefs in Georgian Folk Tales* and a Professor of Philology at Tbilisi State University) with the aid of an interpreter on the third of August 2005, she pointed out to me in the course of our conversation that the suggestion the story might be based on a shamanic journey would of course not have been acceptable in Soviet times and was consequently not one she had ever considered before, though she agreed it was a distinct possibility.

Choloq'ashvili herself refers to three types of folktale that can be found in the Georgian tradition – animal tales, fairy-tales, and what she refers to as "novelistic" tales. "A character of an animal tale fights to get some food; a character of a fairy tale fights to find a fiancée; and a character of a novelistic tale strives for a tremendous property" (Choloq'ashvili, 2004, p.183). Our tale would initially seem to fit into the second of these categories. She goes on to add that "In spite of the differences between these subgenres on the whole they have a common plot: the hero goes to get a marvellous thing, overcomes obstacles three times, gets the desired thing and returns as a winner" (Choloq'ashvili, 2004, p.189). Further observations Choloq'ashvili makes are that "It is inconceivable to end a fairy-tale with the death of the hero" (Choloq'ashvili, 2004, p.187), and that characteristic of the fairy-tale too is the "rewarding of a customs keeper, as well as punishment of a customs infringer [the *dev* in this case]" (Choloq'ashvili, 2004, p.187).

In other respects though, as we have already seen, *The Tale of the Hunter and the Giant Eagle* is very much a shamanic story. Consider, for example, the process of initiation the hunter's son goes through during the course of the tale in the same way as an apprentice shaman would. The term "initiation" can be used to denote

> a body of rites and oral teachings whose purpose is to produce a decisive alteration in the religious and social status of the person to be initiated. In philosophical terms, initiation is equivalent to a basic change in existential condition; the novice emerges from his ordeal endowed with a totally different being from that which he possessed before his initiation; he has become another (Eliade, 1958, p.x).

Eliade believed "myths and fairy tales were derived from, or give symbolic expression to, initiation rites or other rites de passage–such as a metaphoric death of an old, inadequate self in order to be reborn on a higher plane of existence" (Bettelheim, 1991, p.35). And a large number of such myths and legends feature a semi-divine woman in the form of a nymph or a fairy who acts as a teacher, helping the hero through the difficulties of what are often initiatory ordeals and by showing him how to gain possession of the symbol of immortality or long life (see Eliade, 1964, p.78). In *The Tale of the Hunter and the Giant Eagle,* it is the *dev's* youngest daughter who plays this role.

So although it can be classified as a fairy tale, it is not at all a typical one, and is a good example of how the categories of epics, myths, parables, fables, fairy and folk tales tend to overlap.

Among people who once believed in shamanism but were later

converted to various world religions, their former practices may be revealed through an analysis of their folklore and folk beliefs, and this can be applied to Georgia. Georgians have officially lived under the ideological influence of Christianity since the fifth century and then, more recently, under the influence of Communism, during which time pagan rites were frowned upon and their practitioners persecuted. Therefore it is hardly surprising few have been able to survive, and those that have tend to be found in the inaccessible mountainous regions. This enables doubters today to say the findings and data are insufficient to show that shamanism even existed in Georgia. However, stories such as *The Tale of the Hunter and the Giant Eagle* and the folk customs still practised today, even by the more sophisticated urbanites, would seem to indicate otherwise.

***

As for the people of Abkhazia, they live in a mountainous region that is situated on the southeastern coast of the Black Sea. The name the Abkhaz call themselves is *apsua* and their ancient territory they call *Ashvy* (the land of the Abkhaz). As for the Abkhaz language, it belongs to the Abkhazo-Adyghian group of the Caucasian family, and there are two dialects: Abzhui and Bzyb.

According to legend, when God was distributing land to all the different peoples of the earth, the Abkhazians were busy entertaining guests at the time. Because it would have been impolite to leave before their guests, the Abkhazians arrived late, and all that God had left by then was some stones. Out of these it is said he created a land of mountains - hard to grow anything on, but very beautiful.

The first written mention of the Abkhaz people is believed to be the note on the *Abesla* tribes living in Asia Minor, found in the records of the Assyrian ruler Tiglath-pileser. The Proto-Abkhaz

> tribes Apsil, Misiman, Abazg, and Svanig were known to the ancient Greek and Roman historians like Hekateus of Miletus, Strabo and Flavius Arrianus. In the 1st century AD the Proto-Abkhaz tribes set up their own principalities that were united with the Cazika Principality in the 4th century. The 7th-8th centuries witnessed the consolidation of the Proto-Abkhaz tribes into the Abkhaz nation (taken from *The Peoples of the Red Book* http://www.eki.ee/books/redbook/abkhaz.shtml [accessed 20/10/08]).

Subsequently, the Abhz nation was incorporated into Georgia, and then subordinated by Turkey, before eventually becoming a Russian protectorate. After the Crimean and Caucasian wars in the mid-nineteenth century, Abkhaz autonomy became unnecessary for the Russian government, so the last Prince Shervashidze was sent into exile, and tsarist power and Russian bureaucracy were established. In February 1921 the Abkhaz SSR was set up, and in December of that year it was incorporated into the Georgian SSR according to the Union treaty (adapted from *The Peoples of the Red Book* http://www.eki.ee/books/redbook/abkhaz.shtml [accessed 20/10/08]).

Although the Georgians claim that Abkhazia is an integral part of their territory, after the conflict that broke out in the summer of 2008, the Russians recognized the independence of Abkahzia. Not wishing to upset either Georgians or Abkhazians, the decision was therefore made to simply present the current situation in factual form,but to include both territories in the same chapter: "Nationalism, when it breaks out around the Black Sea, is usually a plague which has arrived from somewhere else, and against that plague there is no known serum. This was the fate of Abkhazia" (Ascherson, 2007, p.245). "While the Abkhasians speak a north Caucasian language, the Mingrelains belong to the Kartvelian linguistic family which also includes Georgian, Svanetian and Lazuri ... Georgian nationalists, obsessed with the danger of

Russian interference, took a harsh line towards their own non-Kartvelian minorities" (Ascherson, 2007, p.246) and this was undoubtedly a factor that led to the current crisis. There were other factors that led to the situation that now exists too.

The Russians, instead of helping the two **neighbors** resolve their differences, exacerbated the situation by deliberately fomenting separatist movements within Georgia. "[W]ith the apparent aim of crippling the reality of Georgian independence and reasserting Moscow's hegemony in the northern Caucasus, the Russians supplied the Abkhazian side with heavy weapons and supported their ground troops with air strikes" (Ascherson, 2007, p.247). And now they clearly intend to use their military presence in Abkhazia, and South Ossetia too, "as a lever to apply pressure on Georgia, part of the wider struggle between Russia and the United States for influence in the southern Caucasus" (Ascherson, 2007, p.249).

Our main interest though, is not in the political situation but in the traces of shamanism that can be found in the folktales and also in the present day practices of the peoples.

Polytheistic rituals and beliefs in Abkhazia are inextricably linked to the structure of the extended family or lineage – in other words, all those who share the same surname. Each lineage has its own sacred place, or *a'nyxa*, and "in the past each lineage had its own protective spirits to whom sacrifices and prayers were made at an annual gathering ... These sacred places are natural locations, high up in the mountains, or in forest groves, by springs or rivers, cliffs or sacred trees" (Rachel Clogg in Hewitt, 1999, p.211). They took the place of a church or a mosque and were places where refuge could be sought.

We know from the writings of Procopius of Caesaria in the sixth century, that groves and trees were at one time worshipped by the people. Even today certain trees, groves, and mountains are sacred to clans and villages and are centers of religious gatherings. They embody the strength of a patrilineal line, its connection to a certain place and to God above. We also know that

> In the past, many families worshipped their ancestors, believing that they were linked with an animal, plant, or element of nature, though all that is left of this today is an indication in some Abkhaz surnames that they may derive from the names of animals or plants. The numerous deities traditionally worshipped by the Abkhaz were also almost all associated with the natural world, or certain animals or elements within it. The 'god of gods' in the Abkhaz pantheon is Ants^{W}a, the creator, in whom all the other gods are contained ... The first toast still to be given at feasts is one to Ants^{W}a, in the form of "Ants^{W}a, you give us the warmth of your eyes" (Rachel Clogg in Hewitt, 1999, p.213).

Other gods include Afa, who rules the thunder and other aspects of the weather; Shasta, protector of blacksmiths and all artisans; Azhveipshaa, the spirit of the forest, wild animals, and hunting; and Aitar, the protector of domestic animals.

When it comes to considering the religious beliefs and practices of the people, the paper 'The Shamaness of the Abkhazians' by Andrejs Johansons [translated from the German by *Park McGinty*] taken from *History of Religions*, Vol. 11, No. 3. (Feb., 1972), pp. 251-256, is of particular interest to us as it focuses on the prominent position which was occupied by the shamaness among the Abkhazians.

In Abhaz, a woman who engaged in prophecy and the art of oracles as well as certain cultic observances was called *acaaju* ("the questioner"). The *acaaju* played an important role in the community and people would travel from far and wide to seek their advice.

> ... The foremost obligation of the *acaaju* was to ascertain who had caused a specific illness in order to find out the necessary

remedies. Sometimes she obtained ecstatic inspiration and cried out the name and the demands of the angered divinity. At other times she went lightly across the room or even sat on a high seat and acted as though she was carrying on a conversation with the divinity, to whom she directed questions and from whom she received answers. After a while, she made known the result. For example, the illness could have been sent by Afy on account of a neglected sacrifice. Another important god from whose wrath the people had to protect themselves was Šesšu (also Šašv or Šašvy-ach-du), the supernatural protector of the smithy or forge. As a rule, this god would grow angry over a false oath which the sick person or some one of his relatives had made in the smithy.

The forge had among the Abkhazians, perhaps to an even greater extent than among several other Caucasian peoples, the character of a cult place. If there was no real forge in the neighborhood, a small "symbolic" one was built in the garden or somewhere in the courtyard and used only for religious purposes.

The Abkhazian blacksmith was not only an artisan, but even more, a representative of Šesšu and the mediator between this god and human beings. He also directed the frequent performances of the oath in Šesšu's name, which were carried out with solemn ceremonies in an exactly prescribed form.

It goes without saying that between the smith and the *acaaju* there was close collaboration. If it was a question of discovering the guilty party who had offended Šesšu with a false oath, the *acaaju* employed not only the methods previously mentioned but also material resources. That is, she spread out beans in front of her, and on the basis of the arrangement of these found out the name of the transgressor. If occasion arose, astrology was also taken into account, thus one more technique of divination in which she had to be skilled.

The divine will being ascertained, the *acaajub* reported what kind of animals were to be brought as expiatory sacrifice. She often carried out the sacrifice herself. Beyond that, she also performed various actions of a magical sort. Thus, for example, she led some domestic animal three times around the sick person, after which it was driven away toward the forest, supposedly carrying the sickness away with it. As payment for her help, the *acaaju* received either the skins of the sacrificial animals and a part of the meat or a rather substantial sum of money. 'The Shamaness of the Abkhazians' by Andrejs Johansons [translated from the German by *Park McGinty*] taken from *History of Religions*, Vol. 11, No. 3. (Feb., 1972), pp. 251-256,

Illnesses could be caused by a whole range of factors apart from the wrath of such gods as Afy and Šesšu. For example, lengthy sufferings with fever were considered to be "caused by the water" and in such cases Dzidlan, the Mistress of the Waters or the Water Mother, was called on for help. And rituals would take place at her place of residence – at a pure sweet water lake or a stream. Another widespread belief was that serious illnesses could be caused by a person entering water the moment when the Rainbow drank from it.

It is interesting to note that the *acaaju* was called by a masculine name during the prophecy, and that she was generally spoken to as if she were a man. A ritual change of sex of this kind is a common accompanying phenomenon of shamanism in many parts of the world, and it can take the form of imitative behavior in which identity with a god or spirit is temporarily supposed to be brought about (adapted from http://www.circassianworld.com/pdf/Shamaness.pdf [accessed 20/10/08]).

As for the folktales from Abkhazia, and the North Caucasus in general, it should be pointed out that they are not just 'something to amuse the children'.

They were traditionally one of the chief forms of entertainment, particularly in the mountain districts, together with music, singing and dancing. At the many feasts (i.e. elaborate meals, with much drinking and toasting), the guests would be expected to make a contribution to the entertainment, possibly in the form of a poem or a story. Relating tales would also be a feature of gatherings for the purpose of communal work. Although the primary purpose may have been entertainment, the stories also had an educational value: to confirm the community values of loyalty, hard work, hospitality and so on (Bgazhba, 1985, p.2)

The story that follows was taken from Bgazhba, Kh.S. (1985) *Abkhazian Tales,* translated from the Russian, with a new Introduction by D.G. Hunt. (Russian edition published by Alashara Publishing House, Sukhumi).

The Youngest Son of the Prince

Listen, listen, the story is beginning! Once there lived in the world a certain aged prince, and he had three sons. He became tired of affairs and decided to take a rest in his old age. The prince built a beautiful palace and said to his sons, "My children, respect my old age, brighten up my declining years. Adorn the palace and, so that the songs of little birds delight my ears, get and bring me the birds of the daughter of the deity Aerg. They are famous for their singing". The old prince knew that he is sending his sons on a difficult mission; but he had the secret thought of testing his sons in order to select a worthy successor to himself.

His sons set off on their travels to fulfil their father's command. They came to a junction of three ways, and each of them proceeded along the way that he chose. The oldest brother walked and was thinking: "An old man's whim has overcome father. He has taken a fancy for the little singing birds, but where can they be obtained? Why don't I hire myself out as a workman and wait a little". And he hired himself to a blacksmith. Nor did the middle brother bother himself for long; he hired himself out to a certain baker.

But the youngest brother walked and walked and reached such wild forests as he had never before seen. In its very depths he suddenly saw that he was in the yard of the witch Arupap. She was sitting under a plane tree and was resting. The young man at once guessed who was before him. He rushed towards the witch and, quickly pronouncing the words: "Whether you eat me, whether you cook me, yet I am your son", he kissed her breast.

The old woman sighed and – khop, she was just on the point of swallowing down the young man, but hearing his words, she said, "It is your good fortune; if it had not been for your words, I would have swallowed you down like a fly. Where is your journey taking you, how can I help you?"

The young man answered, "My father has built a beautiful palace, and he has sent me and my two brothers to obtain for him the singing birds of the daughter of Aerg [a deity of hunting]. He wants, in his old age, to delight his ears with their wonderful singing".

The old woman became thoughtful, and then she said, "Your father has given you a difficult task, but I will help you. The biggest difficulty is to make your way through to the birds without being noticed. They sit in a cage. It is necessary to open twelve locked doors. In the last room the beauty is sleeping, and above her head is hanging the golden cage with the birds. The keys of all the rooms are to be found in her pocket. Take down the cage and take it away with you, but so that the beauty does not chase after you, lock all the doors after you".

"But how on earth am I going to pass through all the rooms, if the beauty is lying in the last room, and she has the keys?" asked the young man.

"Go into the mountains, kill a deer and bring it to me", said the witch. "I will make the keys from its bones".

Without lingering to think about it, the young man set off

into the mountains, and since he was an expert hunter, he quickly tracked and killed a deer. He brought it to the witch. She ate all the meat, but from the bones she made twelve keys and gave them to the young man.

Soon the young man found the palace that the witch had spoken to him about. With the bone keys he quietly unlocked all twelve doors, and in the room beyond the last one he saw a sleeping beauty, and above her head – the singing birds in a golden cage. The young man fell in love with the sleeping beauty. She really pleased him a lot; but he had to carry out the business for which his father had sent him. Quietly he took down the cage and left. He locked all the doors after him.

He is riding on the way back. And here is the road junction where the brothers had separated. The youngest brother decided to pay a visit to his older brothers. He quickly found the oldest one at the blacksmith's, and then the middle one at the baker's. He took them with him, and they set out home to their father, to give him pleasure with the singing birds. They rode and they rode, they got tired and hot, they became thirsty. They rode up to a chasm, and they see that down below a spring is gurgling. "Lower me down on a rope, I will collect water", said the young man. No sooner said than done. The youngest brother descended to the spring, collected some cool clear water and shouted, "Haul up the pitcher!"

The older and the middle brothers drank their fill, they looked at each other, and one and the same thought came into each of their heads: "Let us leave our youngest brother here to perish, and we will bring the birds to father. The honour and praise will be for us". And that is just what they did. The young man called and called to his older brothers, but their trail had already gone cold. They abandoned him and did not let down the rope: it was just left up above.

At this time the daughter of Aerg woke up, she looks, and the birds are not there. She jumps and sets off in pursuit of the thief.

She gallops along, and her animals point out the road where the thief has ridden with her birds. So she rides up to the chasm. She hears somebody shouting down below. She let down the rope into the chasm and helped the young man to get out. He recognised her, but said nothing. They rode on further together, and all of the forest beasts and animals point out to the beauty the road where her birds had been taken. And so they reached the prince's palace, and there the people had already gathered, they were all rejoicing at the return of the elder and middle brothers with the birds.

"Who stole my little birds?" asked the daughter of Aerg.

"It was I", said the oldest brother and he proudly stepped out in front of the crowd.

"How exactly did you take them?"

"I broke open all the doors and made off with the cage".

The daughter of Aerg frowned menacingly. "Lock this liar in the stable!" The people did not dare to disobey her and they locked the oldest brother in the stable.

Once again she asks, "Who stole my little birds?"

"I", answered the middle brother. There was no escape for him, willy-nilly he had to answer. After all, he had brought the birds together with his older brother.

"How did you do it?" asked the daughter of Aerg.

"I climbed in the window".

"You are lying too", said the daughter of Aerg. "Lock him in the stable too. So who, then, really did steal my little birds?"

Then the youngest brother came out and said, "It was I who did it". And he related how, with the help of the witch Arupap, he had managed to obtain the wonderful birds.

"Since you succeeded in accomplishing such a feat, then I will marry you, if you are not against it", said she.

Of course the young man was not against it. Aerg's daughter was a marvellous beauty. When the prince found out the whole truth, he ordered that his eldest and middle sons should be driven from the limits of his princedom, but the youngest son he kept for himself. Then they celebrated a merry wedding. I was at the wedding too, and I drank plenty of wine. Although I was drunk, I did not forget this true story, and I told it to you, so that you would know, you young people, how you must fulfil your fathers' wishes.

***

> Many visitors have remarked on the importance of song, music and dance in Abkhazia. There are songs for all occasions: joyous songs for weddings, ritual songs, cult songs, lullabies, healing songs, and work songs [just as there are in neighboring Georgia]. There are special songs for the gathering of the lineage, for a dancing bear, for someone who has measles or St. Vitus' dance; songs celebrating the exploits of heroes, or historical and revolutionary events; humorous songs and contemporary ones. It is believed that hunters must sing their song before leaving for a hunt, or they will not catch anything. … Songs are used like medicine. When someone takes sick, his relatives, in addition to assuming his responsibilities, surround his bed during the night and tell him jokes and stories and sing and dance, in order to take his thoughts away from the pain (Benet, 1974, pp.95-97).

In view of the importance attached to song and music among the Abkhazians, the prince's request for the birds of the daughter of the deity Aerg is thus not as strange as it might at first seem to be.

As is so often the case in the tales from the region, the number three features once again, with the aged prince having three sons, and once again it is the youngest of the three who, by the end of the story, proves to be his worthy successor.

Along the way, the youngest son comes up against the witch Arupap, but by kissing her breast he becomes her son, and so avoids getting swallowed down like a fly by her. She then agrees to become his helper. To reach the birds his father is after, he is required to open twelve locked doors. These represent the barrier that has to be crossed by the shaman when traveling between worlds, and the breakthrough between the planes that accompanies the shamanic process. The shamanic journey frequently involves passing through some kind of gateway, and this serves to represent the insurmountable difficulties of passage to the Other World (see Eliade, 2003, pp.64-65). To make such a journey requires a change in one's mode of being, entering a transcendent state, which makes it possible to attain the world of spirit. Although there is no indication in this particular tale that such a change of state was effected, that is not to assume that it did not. The storyteller might simply have chosen to omit it.

Ritual sucking at the breast of the head female of a family is a well-known procedure in the Caucasus for the adoption of a person into the family. It was also one of the traditional ways of putting an end to a blood feud.

> In the last century, when a son was born to the ruler of the Karakaitags, he was sent from village to village to be suckled by all the women who could, in order to make him foster-brother of his entire generation. This was often a stronger tie than blood; Steder, a traveller-scholar of German origin, writing in 1797 noted that an Ingush murderer suckled his victim's mother at knifepoint, and so became part of her family, to avoid death by the blood-feud. Not long later, the Russian Karginov heard of an Ossete adulterer, who had been forced to kiss the breast of his beloved by her family, to terminate their relationship by making it incestuous (Chenciner, 1997, p.81).

It is interesting to note how Arupap makes full use of the deer she asks the youngest son to kill for her – first by first eating all the meat, and then by using the bones to make the twelve keys he needs. No doubt the skin of the animal was put to good use too. This was of course what our ancestors did, making sure nothing went to waste, a far cry from the way most of us conduct our lives in this day and age.

At a chasm, where down below a spring is gurgling, in other words at a place of power and the equivalent of the world axis where the world pole can be found, the young man asks his brothers to lower him down by means of a rope into what is in effect the lower world. The two brothers do as he requests but then decide to leave him stranded there so that they can claim all the honor and praise for returning to their father with the birds.

It is the daughter of Aerg, while searching for the thief, who helps the youngest son to get out of the hole and so return to this reality, and all of the forest beasts and animals then point out to the beauty the road where her birds can be found. The ability to communicate with the animals and to speak their language, as has already been pointed out in connection with other tales in this volume, is of course one of the traditional attributes of the shaman.

Then, back at the palace, the lies of the older two brothers are exposed and the beauty, on learning that it was in fact the youngest son who succeeded in taking the birds, offers to marry him. The aged prince thus finds his successor and the danger posed to the community by the two older brothers is removed by their banishment from the princedom.

The lesson to be learnt by young people from the tale, we are told by the storyteller, is of the importance of fulfilling their fathers' wishes. In other words, they are expected to follow convention and so maintain the status quo. This was in effect what the shaman was traditionally responsible for seeing to, by the journeys to the spirits he or she undertook on behalf of the members of the community.

In this story it is the youngest son, aided by Arupap, who assumes the role of the shaman, and by marrying the daughter of Aerg he takes on her powers too.

Chapter 6

North Ossetia

First of all, some background information on Ossetia and the Ossetians (The source for much of this information was North Ossetia-Alania-Wikipedia, the free encyclopedia en.wikipedia .org/wiki/North_Ossetia-Alania [accessed 22/6/08]).

North Ossetia-Alania is one of the sovereign republics of the Russian Federation and is situated on the northern slopes of the central Caucasus between two of the highest mountain peaks in Europe, Elbrous (5613m) and Kazbeck (5047m). It is one of the smallest, most densely populated and multi-cultural republics, with an area of 8,000 square kilometers (3,088.8 sq ml), and a population of 710,275 in 2002, representing about 100 different nationalities.

As for the people, they are "the distant descendants and last representatives of the northern Iranians whom the ancients called Scythians and Sarmatians and who, at the dawn of the Middle Ages, under the name of the Alani and Roxolani, made Europe quake with fear" (Bonnefoy, 1993, p.262).

The ancestors of the Ossetians were the Alans, and the Daryal Gorge takes its name from them ("Dar-i-Alan", Gate of the Alans). They wandered as nomads over the steppes watered by the Terek, Kuban and Don Rivers until the Huns, under Attila, swept into Europe and split them into two parts. One group of the Alans moved into Western Europe; along with another wandering people, the Vandals, they passed through Spain into North Africa, where they disappear from history (Pearce, 1954, p.12). The other group were forced southwards and eventually settled along the Terek, immediately north of the main Caucasus Range. There they entered into trading and cultural relations with other people of the Black Sea region, and in the tenth century were converted to Christianity. "[T]hough they did not in this period attain to a written literature, the Ossetians evolved a remarkable saga, passed down orally from generation to generation-the saga of the Narts, semi-mythical heroes, something like King Arthur's Knights" (Pearce, 1954, p.12).

The vast epic cycle of the Narts is noteworthy in several respects, in particular as it is probably the last great European epic still alive and flourishing today. Not only that, but it also provides us with entire sections of a mythology that would otherwise have been lost to us.

The Narts are heroes of the past, simultaneously earthly and miraculous, who are distinguished by supernatural qualities (steel body, magic power, superhuman strength, etc.) but who lead the same daily lives as Caucasian warriors with their houses, customs, and passions. Like them, they love to talk and fight, and divide their time among feasts, raids, and war, the very image of the northern Caucasus before the Russian conquest. The Nart epic is as richly represented among the Circassians and the Abkhazians as it is among the Ossets … But its Ossetic, even Indo-European, origin is beyond doubt (Bonnefoy, 1993, p.263)

In the last years of the Soviet Union, as nationalist movements swept throughout the Caucasus, many intellectuals in the North Ossetian ASSR called for the revival of the name of Alania, a medieval kingdom of the Alans, ancestors of the modern-day Ossetians. The term "Alania" quickly became popular in Ossetian daily life, so much so that in November 1994, "Alania" was added to the official name, which became the Republic of North Ossetia-Alania.

The population of North Ossetia today is predominantly Christian with a large Muslim minority, speaking Ossetic and Russian. According to the 2002 Census, Ossetians make up 62.7% of the republic's population. Other groups include Russians (23.2%), Ingush (3.0%), Armenians (2.4%), Kumyks (12,659, or 1.8%),

Georgians (10,803, or 1.5%), Ukrainians (0.7%), and Chechens (3,383, or 0.5%). Despite the predominant religion being Russian Orthodox Christianity, followed by Islam, many of the native rituals predate both faiths.

The most popular element of the animist-pagan tradition is the cult of Wasterzhi and his sacred grove about 30 kilometers from the capital Vladikavkaz. Part protector of warriors and travelers, part phallic symbol, Wasterzhi is a mysterious character whose origins have been linked to Indo-Iranian sun worship, star worship, war gods and the ancient Nart heroes of the Caucasus. A painting often seen reproduced on posters depicts him as a medieval knight with a long beard on a white stallion with sizeable testicles.

Hoping to fully convert the Ossetians, the Russian Orthodox Church encouraged Christian saints as replacements for Wasterzhi and the rest of the extensive pagan pantheon, headed by Khusaw, the Almighty. But instead of abandoning their gods, the Ossetians fused them with the saints, creating hybrid deities subservient to Khusaw and Christianity's God. Wasterzhi's alter ego was Saint George, and Wasilla, the god of harvests and thunder, became interchangeable with Saint Illya.

No priests are required in the popular Ossetian faith. Against a background of heavy feasting and many religious vodka toasts, Ossetian families and villages will sacrifice sheep and bulls to these lesser divinities and implore their help (Smith, 2006, p.81). The first toast is always to the head god, who is known as "Khutsauty Khutsau ('god of gods'), or simply Khutsau, like Anc°a among the Abkhasians or Morige among the Georgians, does not intervene directly in human affairs but delegates his powers to minor deities" (Bonnefoy, 1993, p.262).

The legend behind the sacred grove outside Vladikavkaz is that a certain Hetag was fleeing his enemies in the 14th to 16th centuries when Wasterzhi called out from the mountain forest and told him to shelter there. Exhausted, Hetag collapsed on the plains, saying he could not go on, whereupon a clump of trees (today's wood) miraculously came down and hid him. ... Ever since, the grove has been a living cathedral for Wasterzhi, a memorial to Hetag, and an open-air chapel for Saint George.

[T]he wood, best known as Hetag's Grove, is deeply venerated. It is largely made up of ashes and beeches, covering just under 13 hectares in a roughly triangular shape. A temple with a large wooden totem pole has been built nearby, alongside a ... banquet hall for the yearly festivals, where each village is assigned its own tree and clearing.

> ...Believers who pass the grove along the main road, about a kilometre away, rise out of their seats and mumble a few prayers to Wasterzhi, while once in the wood it is forbidden to break off even a single branch. Holy trees are decorated with ribbons and portraits of Saint George and the dragon. And because of his fertility powers, women are forbidden from saying either Hetag or the W word (Smith, pp.81-82).

When atheism was in force in Soviet times, there was a real barrier to local traditions, but even then, the head of household would still gather his family and pray to Wasterzhi and drink a toast, and the tradition has both survived and flourished against all the odds.

Despite the inevitable economic burden of a sizeable refugee population, North Ossetia is the most well-to-do republic in the northern Caucasus. It is the most urbanized and the most industrialized, with factories producing metals (lead, zinc, tungsten, etc.), electronics, chemicals, and processed foods. The Republic also has abundant mineral resources and its numerous mountain rivers serve as an important source of electric power. More than half of the territory of the Republic is occupied by high mountains, rich in deciduous and coniferous woods, as well as alpine pastures. The territory of North Ossetia has been inhabited for thousands of years by the Vainakh tribes, being both a very fertile agricultural region and a key trade route through the Caucasus Mountains. The ancestors of the present inhabitants were a people called the Alans, a warlike nomadic people who spoke an Iranian language. Part of the Alan people eventually settled in the Caucasus around the 7th century AD. By about the 9th century, the kingdom of Alania had arisen and had been converted to Christianity by Byzantine missionaries. Alania became a powerful state in the Caucasus, profiting greatly from the legendary Silk Road to China, which passed through its territory.

Polytheism is characteristic of the world of beliefs of nomads, and the Samartian Alans were no exception to this. Batraz was the Alan god of war, and there was also a mother goddess who was the equivalent of the Greek Potnia Théron. As for the cult of the Sun and the Moon, beside altars dated from the end of the 6th and the beginning of the 5th centuries BC, smoking vessels have been found. It is highly likely that the people who took part in the rituals would have been overcome by the smoke produced from these vessels, and that this could have resulted in them entering altered states of consciousness, which is of course what shamans frequently did (see Vaday, 2002, pp.215-221).

From the Middle Ages onwards, Alania was beset by external enemies and, due to its strategic geographical position, suffered repeated invasions. The invasions of the Mongols and Tatars in the 13th century decimated the population, who were now known as Ossetians. Islam was introduced in the 17th century through the Kabardians, a Muslim Caucasian people. Incursions by the Khanate of Crimea and the Ottoman Empire eventually pushed Alania/Ossetia into an alliance with Russia in the 18th century. North Ossetia was among the first areas of the northern Caucasus to come under Russian domination, starting in 1774, and the capital, Vladikavkaz, was the first Russian military outpost in the region. By 1806, Ossetia was completely under Russian control.

The arrival of the Russians led to the rapid development of the region, with industries founded and road and rail connections built to overcome Ossetia's isolation. The Georgian Military Road, which is still a crucial transport link across the mountains, was built in 1799 and a railway line was built from Vladikavkaz to Rostov-on-Don in Russia proper. The Ossetians' traditional culture inevitably underwent some russification, but their new connections with Russia and the West helped to boost local culture; the first books in the Ossetian language were printed in the late 18th century. Ossetia became part of the Terskaya Region of Russia in the mid-19th century.

After the Russian Revolution, North Ossetia became part of the short-lived Soviet Mountain Republic in 1921. It became the North Ossetian Autonomous Oblast on July 7, 1924 and was then made the North Ossetian Autonomous Soviet Socialist Republic (ASSR), within the Russian Soviet Federated Socialist Republic, on December 5, 1936.

During and after the war Stalin undertook massive deportations of whole ethnicities explaining this by anti-Sovietism, separatism and collaboration with Nazi Germany. In particular, this affected Balkars, Chechens, and Ingush. As of 1944, the part of the Prigorodny District on the right bank of the Terek River had been part of Chechen-Ingush SSR, but it was granted to North Ossetia following Stalin's deportation of the Chechens and Ingush to Central Asia. Although they were eventually allowed to return from exile, they were generally not allowed to settle in the original territories.

North Ossetian SSR finally became the first autonomous republic of the RSFSR to declare national sovereignty, on June 20, 1990 (although it still remains firmly part of Russia). In 1991 it was renamed the Republic of North Ossetia-Alania.

The dissolution of the Soviet Union posed particular problems for the Ossetian people, who were divided between North Ossetia, which was part of the Russian SFSR, and South Ossetia, part of the Georgian SSR. In December 1990 the Supreme Soviet of Georgia abolished the autonomous Ossetian enclave amid the rising ethnic tensions in the region, and much of the population fled across the border to North Ossetia or Georgia proper. Some 70,000 South Ossetian refugees were resettled in North Ossetia, sparking clashes with the predominantly Ingush population in the Prigorodny District. That led to Ossetian-Ingush conflict.

As well as dealing with the effects of the conflict in South Ossetia, North Ossetia has also had to deal with refugees and the occasional spillover of fighting from the war in neighboring Chechnya. The bloodiest incident by far was the September 2004 Beslan hostage crisis, in which Chechen Muslim separatists of Shamil Basayev seized control of a school. In the firefight between the terrorists and Russian forces that ended the crisis, 335 civilians, the majority of them children, died.

So the Ossetes today are a divided people, with one group (Kudakhtsy) living in South Ossetia (Georgia) and the majority living in North Ossetia (Russia). The latter are comprised of two ethnic sub-groups, Irontsy and Digortsy, each of them possessing their own dialect. North Ossetia … was renamed 'North Ossetia-Alania' in 1994 with an aspiration to drop 'North Ossetia' at some stage, so that remaining 'Alania' would include both the South and the North (Matveena, 1999, p.89).

However, in the summer of 2008, everything changed. For on 7 August, after a series of low-level clashes in the region, Georgia tried to retake South Ossetia by force. Russia launched a counter-attack and the Georgian troops were ousted from both South Ossetia and Abkhazia. This was followed by Russia recognizing the independence of the two breakaway regions. The rest of the world, however, has not followed suit, and what the future will bring remains uncertain at this point.

Apparently, prior to the conflict breaking out, the US had warned Georgia that Russia was baiting them, and that a military response would only play into Moscow's hands, but they nevertheless went ahead and launched the offensive that led to the current state of affairs. Therefore, in a sense it can be argued that they only have themselves to blame for what has transpired. The fact that Georgia has a staunch nationalist as a President, in the form of Saakashvili, probably did not help matters either. On the other hand, if Russia had not stirred up discontent in the region in the first place, the South Ossetians and the Georgians could well be living peacefully side by side now.

One of the reasons why nationalism plays such an important role in Georgian politics is that it has provided the basic vocabulary through which political opposition has been expressed (see King, 2008, p.214). The focus has been, and still is, on gathering in the lands that supposedly once belonged to an older state, even though, in reality, "the idea of a Georgian nation stretching back into the mists of time is as ephemeral as all ideologies of the nation" (King, 2008, pp.178-179).

***

The Rich Man and the Poor Man

There was once a poor man and his wife. A rich man said to him one day, "Come, poor wretch, I will take you out hunting with me." "How can I go hunting with you," the poor man replied, "when I have no food to take with me?" "Tell your wife she must beg for a bowl of flour and bake provisions for your journey." So the poor man went to his wife and explained the matter to her; she went out begging, brought home a bowl of flour and baked bread for her husband.

The following day the rich man and the poor man went hunting together. They wandered about all day, but saw no game. In the evening they looked out a place to spend the night, lighted a fire and sat down. They sat there a long time, at last the poor man said it must be time for supper. "Yes, you are right," answered the rich man. They took out what they had brought, ate their supper and then lay down to sleep. The next day again they saw no game and returned at night to their former camp. Again they sat there for a long time till the poor man again thought of food. "But what shall we eat?" asked the rich man. "Have you perhaps still some food?" – pulled out his own provisions and ate, but gave the poor man nothing. He looked on while the other satisfied his hunger, and as he saw that nothing was intended for him, he asked for a morsel. "If you allow me to put out one of your eyes, then I will give you something to eat," answered the rich man. What could the poor man do? There was nothing for it but to sacrifice his eye, for which he received a piece of bread. But he had hardly eaten it before the rich man said: "Get away from here! Your misfortune has depressed me," and drove him away. He would not even allow him to spend the night there. The poor man groped his way through the wood during the night and came at last to an open field where he saw a light at the foot of a little hill, and went towards it. As he drew nearer he saw a house before him. He looked in, and as he found it was empty he crawled up among the rafters and hid himself there. Soon afterwards a wolf, a bear and a fox arrived and came into the house. The bear said to the others: "We live together and we sleep together, then why should we not also eat together? Let each of us bring out what he has."

"All that I have," said the fox, "is a piece of gold cloth. That is all I possess, I live by it, I eat and drink by it. I only need to shake it once or twice and all sorts of things to eat and drink fall out of it." "That is certainly an invaluable possession, fox," said the bear; "but I have a whole pit full of gold. Yes, that is what I have; just come with me and I will show it to you." The wolf pointed to a tree and said, "When I steal a sheep and am wounded I run to this tree and rub myself upon it, and my wounds heal up at once as if nothing had happened to me."

In this way the three shared all their possessions and all their powers in common. But the bear was a clever beast. "If we use up all that we have," he said, "what will happen to us? It will be better to work. What will you do?" "I will go and bring in hens," said the fox. "And I will go and fetch a sheep," said the wolf, and "I will go and eat oats," said the bear.

They arranged all that at night, and in the morning each set out to do what he had planned. But our poor man was still up among the rafters. When the three had gone away he climbed down, took everything that belonged to the bear and the fox, the cloth of gold and the money, went to the tree the wolf had spoken of and rubbed his face where his eye had been put out. At once he saw again as well as before. Then he went on and came to a shepherd who asked him what he was carrying on his back. "Nothing special," he answered, "I was hunting with the rich man, what could I have but cabbages?"

In the meantime the wolf had come up, and called out to the shepherd he should hand over the tribute he owed him. "Just come here," the shepherd called to him, and the wolf slunk up to the flock, nearer and nearer. But the shepherd shot at him with such good aim that his brains fell out of his skull. The poor man took the brains—he said to the shepherd it was a cure for certain illnesses—and stuck them in his knapsack. The wolf ran to his tree and rubbed himself upon i—but this time it did not cure him; the tree had used up all its magic powers on the poor man! He travelled on till he came to a village that belonged to a prince.

Now this prince was very ill and from all quarters people were coming—as the custom is—to visit him. The poor man asked them why they had all gathered there, and when he heard the reason he expressed his desire to visit the prince himself. At first they would not allow him, but the prince had heard of his wish and gave orders that he was to be allowed in. The poor man came into the prince's room, sat down and said, according to the custom, "May the power of a living man be granted to you." Then he asked the sick man what remedies were being used. "Ah," he answered, "if only I knew somebody who would bring me a good remedy, I would give him whatever he asked." The poor man had some milk brought in, boiled the wolf's brain in it, and gave the sick man some of the soup to drink, and the prince became well instantly—he felt as strong as a stag. And he did not stint his thanks; he had his horses brought in from the meadow, chose out the best horse, saddled it, took his best sabre, his best dagger, his best gun and his best pistol and gave them all to the poor man. When he was already mounted on the horse to ride away, the prince presented him with a whole flock of sheep with its shepherds. And the poor man rode off as fast as the wind.

When the rich man heard of all this, he went to meet the poor man and asked him where he had got all his riches.—"Tell me quickly, or I will take half of them away from you," he threatened; "we were together, you know." "If you let me put out one of your eyes I will tell you," answered the poor man. Well, there seemed no way out of it; the rich man held out his face and the poor man put out his eye with the dagger he had received from the prince. Then he said, "When I left you that night, I saw a light, went towards it and came to a hill where a bear, a wolf, and a fox lived. I got all that I have from them." The rich man set out at once, found the house, and hid himself among the rafters. The three came home towards evening, first of all the wolf, who did not seem very well. When they were all three together and had rested a little, the bear asked, "Well, which of you has brought home anything?"

"I went to the shepherds," said the wolf, "and was wounded. Then I ran to my tree and rubbed and rubbed myself upon it, but in vain—that is why I am not well." "And I," said the fox, "I went to all the hen-houses but could get nothing." "And I," added the bear, "I wanted to eat oats but it was still green, and so I too have come home empty." They sat there a long while, till it was time for supper. Then the bear told the fox to go and prepare something to eat and drink. The fox lighted a candle and looked for his cloth of gold, but could not find it anywhere. "Ah, you are only teasing us," said the bear; "I will go and fetch a rouble out of my pit." But the pit was empty! "I am ill and know nothing about it!" said the wolf. "No, no, it must have been you. You are just pretending to be ill so that we may not suspect you, but you cannot deceive us that way," cried the bear, and he and the fox threw themselves on the wolf. They killed him and ate him up.

When they were finished, the fox sprang up among the rafters to look for his cloth of gold, and there he found the rich man. "Here is a man," he cried down to the bear; "he has hidden himself here. He is the thief, and we have killed our companion for nothing."

And they dragged the rich man down, and ate him up in spite of all his assurances that he was not the thief.

But God had appointed a happy life for the poor man, and he lives to this day (taken from Dirr. A. (1925) *Caucasian Folk-tales*, translated into English by Lucy Menzies, London & Toronto: J.M. Dent & Sons Ltd.).

***

The style of storytelling employed is once again that of magic realism, a fusion of logic and "nonsense", in which the logic is satisfied by the factual information provided. As for the magic, it sets in when the rich man asks the poor man to sacrifice one of his eyes for something to eat, and he receives nothing more than a piece of bread for it.

The reason why the rich man asks for an eye rather than any

other part of the body could have something to do with the ancient and widespread belief that certain people have the power to harm or even kill just with a glance, and that various means, such as the use of charms or gestures, could be employed to counteract its effects. For example, Virgil speaks of an evil eye bewitching lambs: "Nescio quis teneros oculus mihi fascinat agnos" (*Bucolics, Ecl.* iii, 103). Belief in "the evil eye" is commonplace in Daghestan too:

> The evil eye was always held to be capable of bewitching and had to be avoided, as it could cause illness or even death. Even today, beads to keep the evil eye at bay are sewn on children's clothing from birth, or worn around their wrists or necks. Small glass beads, resembling eyes, were favoured by the Dargins, as were the bones or teeth of boar, fox, wolf or goat, sea shells, bears' claws, and egg shells. The Lezgins protected themselves with amulets in red cloth bags or leather pouches, adapted in Muslim times to hold a few lines from the Koran, sewn into their clothing. Richer folk would keep an amulet box, containing barley, apricot kernels, quince or cornelian cherry, as fruit-bearing plants were thought to have healing properties (Chenciner, 1997, p.86).

In the case of indigenous shamanism,

> the chief methods of recruiting shamans are: (1) hereditary transmission of the shamanic profession and (2) spontaneous vocation ("call" or "election"). ... However selected, a shaman is not recognized as such until after he has received two kinds of teaching: (1) ecstatic (dreams, trances, etc.) and (2) traditional (shamanic techniques, names and functions of the spirits, mythology and genealogy of the clan, secret language, etc.) (Eliade, 1989, p.13).

Receiving the shamanic "call" would traditionally lead to an initiatory journey that often required some form of sacrifice or dismemberment, and the poor man's loss of an eye represents this. The result is that he then finds he understands the language of the animals, who act inadvertently as his helpers.

The process of dismemberment culminating in consumption can be seen as a survival from the hunting phase, since it mirrors what a hunter does to his quarry;

> namely kills it, skins it, removes the offal, then cooks and eats it ... By offering himself as a sacrificial victim the shaman is repaying the debt humans have incurred by their slaughter of animals. In the words of Rasmussen's Eskimo, "All the creatures we have to kill and eat, all those we have to strike down and destroy to make clothes for ourselves, have souls, as we have" (Rutherford, 1986, p.37).

However,

> As with every other detail of the shaman's calling, the death/rebirth cycle, though constant, shows regional variations so that in some places it is reduced to the symbolical form of an initiatory rite. In others, the extreme opposite applies and the candidate may have to undergo ordeals of an extremely painful nature, either self-inflicted or inflicted by initiators (Rutherford, 1986, p.38).

Ordeals the apprentice may be required to undergo in non-ordinary reality during his/her initiation can include torture and violent dismemberment of the body, the scraping away of the flesh until the body is reduced to a skeleton, the substitution of viscera and renewal of the blood, and even a period spent in Hell during which the future shaman is taught by the souls of dead shamans and by demons (see Eliade, 2003, p.96).

The shamanic journey frequently involves passing through

some kind of gateway. As Eliade explains:

> The "clashing of rocks," the "dancing reeds," the gates in the shape of jaws, the "two razor-edged restless mountains," the "two clashing icebergs," the "active door," the "revolving barrier," the door made of the two halves of the eagle's beak, and many more–all these are images used in myths and sagas to suggest the insurmountable difficulties of passage to the Other World [and sometimes the passage back too] (Eliade, 2003, pp.64-65). And to make such a journey requires a change in one's mode of being, entering a transcendent state, which makes it possible to attain the world of spirit. (Berman, 2007, p.48).

In this particular story, passing through some kind of gateway can be seen to take place when the poor man crawls up into the rafters in the house upon the hill, with the rafters representing the barrier between the two worlds.

One of the attributes traditionally associated with shamans is their ability to communicate with animals who act as their helpers, and in this particular tale the fox, the bear, and the wolf fulfill the role.

The fox has a piece of gold cloth that only needs to be shaken to produce all the food and drink you could ever wish for; the bear has a pit that produces a seemingly bottomless supply of gold; and the wolf knows of a tree that has healing properties. The poor man learns of these things by listening to the animals' conversation and then avails himself of what they have to offer.

When the wolf is shot through the head by a shepherd, the poor man asks for, and is given, the animal's brains, which he boils in milk and uses to treat a prince who happens to be the owner of a village he travels to. The poor man succeeds where all others have failed and is well rewarded for his efforts. The rich man, learning of the poor man's good fortune, seeks the same and so threatens him in order to discover the secret behind his success. As the rich man acts with the wrong intent, though, the information he is given just leads to his downfall.

Although emphasis is often placed on the healing of individual illness, either psychological or physical, it should be remembered that another role the shaman can play is in the healing of the community, and the poor man in our story, as well as having his own sight restored, achieves this by his actions too. For not only does he succeed in restoring the health of the prince on whom the future prospects of the community rests, but he also rids society of the danger the rich man poses.

Not surprisingly, it is the fox that ultimately discovers the rich man hiding in the rafters and ensures that justice prevails:

> The fox is agile, bright and brave, so eases out of awkward situations and wins out over the stronger animals, such as wolves, bears, leopards and lions. The fox stands for people who are swift to recognise social injustice. So, in a struggle with her stronger enemies the fox is sure to win, whereas weaker opponents always triumph over her. The fox is crafty, not only fooling animals but people as well (Chenciner, 1997, p199).

The role played by all three animals in the tale, not just the fox, offers evidence to indicate that ancient totemistic ideas and beliefs clearly lie behind the story. Support for this hypothesis is provided above all by cultic concepts with magical functions, like the belief that rubbing against a tree can heal wounds, for example. The importance accorded to the magical properties of trees in the region has already been referred to in connection with the legend behind the sacred grove outside Vladikavkaz.

Finally, the question has to be asked why the poor man agreed to go hunting with the rich man in the first place when he must have know that risks were involved. Perhaps what the poor man had in effect was nostalgia for an initiatory renewal. Nostalgia for an initiatory renewal can be regarded as "the modern formulation of man's eternal longing to find a positive meaning in death, to accept death as a transition rite to a higher mode of being ... not subject to the destroying actions of Time" (Eliade, 2003, p.136). Indeed, it can be argued that it is only in initiation that death is given a positive value. And in our present day and age, the practitioners of neo-shamanism, by attempting to make the techniques accessible to everyone rather than just an elite few, would claim that they thus enable us to experience such a process for ourselves.

Chapter 7

Daghestan

Known as the "land of the mountains," Daghestan lies immediately north of the Caucasus Mountains, and stretches for approximately 250 miles along the west shore of the Caspian Sea.

With its mountainous terrain making travel and communication difficult, Daghestan is still largely tribal and, unlike in most other parts of Russia, the population (2,576,531 in 2002) is rapidly growing. Despite over a century of Tsarist control followed by seventy years of repressive Soviet rule and russification policies, there are still 32 distinct ethnic groups, each with its own language, and Avar is the most widely spoken with about 700,000 speakers. With so many indigenous ethnic groups, Daghestan is unquestionably the most complex of the Caucasian republics.

In the lowlands can be found Turkic nomads: Kumyks, Noghays, and a few displaced Turkomans. In the northern highlands are the Avars, the Andis, Karatas, Chamalals, Bagwalals, Akhwakhs, Botlikhs, Godoberis, and Tindis. Still in the high valleys but going south towards the Georgian border are the Tsez (Dido), Ginukhs, Hunzibs, Khwarshis, and Bezhitas (Kapuchis). South of the Avar are the Laks, Dargwas, Kubachis, and Khaidaqs, all forming a related group of peoples. In one high village, standing apart from them, are the Archis, whose links lie further south with the so-called Lezgian peoples: the Aghuls, Tabasarans, and Rutuls. A few of the Lezgis and most of the Tsakhurs spill over into Azerbaijan in the south. Other Daghestanis who are restricted to northern Azerbaijan are the Kryz in one mountain village and three coastal ones, Budukhs (one mountain village), Udis (two mountain villages), and Khinalugs (one mountain village). There is also a group called "Mountain Jews" (Givrij or Dagchifut) who speak an

Iranian language in Daghestan. They are sometimes called "Tats," but are not to be confused with the Muslim Tats further south on the Apsheron peninsula of Azerbaijan. In addition there are a few Daghestani Cossacks who are strongly assimilated to indigenous patterns.

Colarusso (1997), who compiled the above list, stresses that all thirty-two

> are distinct peoples, however small they may be, with their own languages, customs, costumes, arts, and architectures. Many are further subdivided by tribes, clans, and blood lines. Conversely, most will traditionally form larger units for self-defence when threatened. This is particularly true of the smaller peoples of Daghestan. In ethnographic, social, and political terms the Caucasus is like a miniature continent.

To give some idea of the problems caused by the linguistic mix, despite the fact that Dargi and Avar are spoken by people living side by side with each other they are in fact mutually incomprehensible languages (see Chenciner et al, 1997, p.9). Multilingualism is therefore virtually universal. Nearly everyone speaks Russian in addition to their own language, and many have some command of several neighboring languages too.

The Avars, incidentally, "are an offshoot of the people of that name who accompanied the Huns in their migration westward, and a small body of whom, bending their course to the south, crossed the Terek, and effected a settlement in the mountains of Daghestan, where their descendents still form a distinct tribe" (Ussher, 1865, p.144). In the eighteenth century, the Avars were the only group in the region to successfully defy the Persian invasion of Nadir Shah, and Shamyl, who fought a religious war so successfully for many years against the Russians in the last century, was also an Avar. Most of the ethnic groups "are subdivided into *tukhums*, or extended family clans, which traditionally did not intermarry and often fought long blood feuds. The *tukhum* managed the village affairs and laws. Today, the *tukhum* still functions as a unit, but to greatly varying degrees among different ethnic groups of the mountain land. [In addition,] ... elders throughout the region play a vital role in ensuring the preservation of traditional rules within the family and, by extension, in society" (Smith, 2006, p.23). In the villages in Daghestan, the clans have their own tea houses in which their members gather.

As is the case throughout the Caucasus, it is the tradition for the eldest man to be master of the extended family unit in so far as he rules over disputes or regulates social relationships with the outside world. Within the confines of the home, however, the eldest woman runs the show.

In Daghestan 93% percent of the population is Muslim, consisting of Sunni Sufi orders that have been in place for centuries, with Christians accounting for much of the remaining 7%. There are also the "Mountain Jews".

According to legend, the *Juhur* as they called themselves, are descended from the ten lost tribes that were exiled from the Kingdom of Israel in the eighth century BC. Although this cannot be verified, we do know there were Jewish communities in the eastern Caucasus as early as the third century AD. They moved there to escape persecution in Persia and brought their own language with them. (see Mikdash-Shamailov, 2002, p.17).

> The language ... is an ethnolect of Tat, which belongs to the southwestern subgroup of the Iranian language. Four local dialects of the ethnolect can be identified: those of Derbent, Kuba, Makhachkala-Nalchik (historically the Haytaghi dialect), and Vartashen – now Oguz (historically, the Shirvani dialect). The usual designation for this ethnolect in the scientific literature is "Judeo-Tat," but the Mountain Jews call it *zuhun juhuri* – literally, "the Jewish language." (Mikdash-Shamailov, 2002, p.37).

Although the Mountain Jews only form a small community these days, at one time Judaism was the predominant religion in the region. The choice of Judaism as the state religion in pagan Khazaria can be explained by the presence in the country of a large local Khazar-Jewish population, of Jewish proselytes among the mountaineers and the Khazars, and by the desire of the Khazar khans themselves to show that they were politically independent of hostile neighboring states, of the Muslim Arab caliphate, and of Christian Byzantium. Another important factor in the acceptance of Judaism by the Khazar khans was the influence of the Jewish aristocracy: merchants, magnates, and rabbis serving at the courts of the Khazar khans as businessmen and advisers. This led to the emergence of a Jewish-Khazar kinship entity.

After the fall of the Khazar Khanate to the Arabs from the south and the Russians from the north towards the end of the tenth century, many Khazar Jews withdrew into the depths of mountainous Daghestan; those who remained in their old haunts found themselves in an oppressive feudal dependency on the Arab rulers of the Caucasus and their local agents. They were forced to bring tribute and other payments, and, to preserve their Jewish faith, to pay a special tax (*j'dzh*); many of them, particularly the converts from among the mountaineers and the Khazars, turned to Islam. The Arab caliphate and their agents were in turn replaced by new conquerors (the Seljuk Turks, the Persian shahs, and Turkish sultans) and a series of Azerbaijani and Daghestani khanates and overlords. In conditions of feudal disintegration, the Mountain Jews found themselves under the control of local rulers with the legal status of dependent peasants. With the unification of Azerbaijan and Daghestan with Russia in 1813, the Mountain Jews accepted Russian citizenship, the status of "Jew" was imposed on them, and they began to be called into military service.

The social oppression of tsarism, to which were added the pogroms, then made life extremely difficult for the Mountain Jews. To compound their problems even further, the White Guard bands of Bicherakov and Denikin, invaded the area in 1918-1920, and were responsible for destruction and looting that led to many of the families migrating to Palestine.

The majority of Mountain Jews today are non-believers, and one of the reasons for the departure from the faith was the increasingly negative attitude in the former Soviet Union as a whole to the Jewish religion, partially in reaction to the creation of the state of Israel. The more conservative elements in the community began to link the leading elements of the Mountain Jewish population with Zionists. This damaged the Jewish ethnic identity, and explains why many Mountain Jews began not only to conceal their Jewish faith but to call themselves "Tat."

The three synagogues in Daghestan (in Derbent, Makhachkala, and Buynaksk) are now only used by a small number of believers, primarily of the older generation, and the faith is mainly maintained through the performance of traditional rituals in the home.

A number of pre-Judaic and pre-monotheistic concepts, including belief in the purifying strength of fire, water, amulets, and talismans against evil spirits (water nymphs, devils, etc.) are still practised by the Mountain Jews too. As for oaths, they "are rendered by the Torah and the Talmud, but also by the hearth," which would be the traditional Daghestani way. (Much of this information on the history and current situation of the Mountain Jews in Daghestan has been adapted from http://www.everyculture.com/Russia-Eurasia-China/Mountain-Jews-Religion.html [accessed 1/8/08]).

For many years the Communist Party in Daghestan waged war against local culture, especially Islamic practices, through the atheistic Society of Godless Zealots. However, despite all their efforts, two Sufi groups are active in both Daghestan and neighboring Chechnya: the Naqshbandis and the Qadiris. They practise the *zikr* chant, and this is how it has been described:

> The hypnotic male chanting, swaying from a single voice to the roar of the whole company was like the sea. Only this was no normal sea: it may have begun there but soon it changed into the waters of the Old Testament Creation which *could* stir the forgotten roots of humanity, releasing unknown powers. The chant took everything along on its path or *tariqat* towards the mystic experience where man communicated directly with God ... After prolonged solemn chanting by the men standing in a stationary ring, they swayed slightly and juddered apparently uncoordinatedly from foot to foot and began their extraordinary movement. Each man stretched his left hand straight down, with the palm horizontal and open. He raised his right hand above his head and brought it down to clap against his left which he did not move. At the same time his right knee jerked up and stomped back on the ground and so the circular movement began, repeated again and again to a new loud rhythmic beat ... They seemed possessed. I was told that women also performed this *zikr* (Chenciner, 1997, p.212)

By "possessed", Chenciner probably means in a trancelike state, which is what shamans traditionally enter – by such means as listening to the sound of a drumbeat, chanting, or by using psychoactive drugs. And it would seem highly unlikely that a culture in which Sufi dancing is widely practised was not at one time a shamanic one.

What we find in Daghestan is very much an amalgam of practices. For example, on tombstones with Arab inscriptions, microcosmic maps can be found similar to those found in Kaitag embroidery. Animist and Islamic iconographies thus exist side by side (see Chenciner, 1997, p.92). And on the day of the new moon before Uraza Bayram at the end of Ramadan, it was customary for people to visit the graves of their ancestors. What this shows is that as in neighboring Chechnya and Azerbaijan too, "there has been an Islamicisation of traditional ancestor-worship" (Chenciner, 1997, p.95).

Even some mosques had pre-Islamic features,

> like the zoomorphic rafter terminals of dragon neck and head shape, rising over the arcade along the front long side of the old mosque in Djuli in Tabassaran. This was similar to other finials on both sides of the surviving pagan shrine at Rekom, near Tsei in North Ossetia, where the sacrificed ram skulls were stacked on shelves against the log cabin walls. The same many-headed motif also appeared on tapestry carpets (Chenciner, 1997, pp.145-146).

Not only have animist practices been incorporated into Islamic ones, but they have also been combined with Soviet rituals, an example of this being the Lezgin Festival of Flowers, *Sukversovar*, which is held in Akhti every June.

> Local boys and girls climbed the mountain peak to gather magic flowers before dawn. They took food and wine and sang and danced all day. The best girl worker in the *kolkhoz* was crowned queen, and danced with a clown in a tall white sheepskin hat, differing from the older version, where a shah would wrestle and fight the clowns with his *kinjal* dagger. Finally, the queen and her attendants rode down the mountain with the flowers to give them to the old villagers for luck. Celebrations continued until midnight. But they now wear foreign costumes, because the festival must be international, and is organised by the Party *khudozhnik samodetni*, or self-action artist (Chenciner, 1997, p.248).

Like all the other nations in the Caucasus, the Daghestanis have long been noted as being "a hospitable people, and whoever breaks bread or eats salt with them is protected and defended with their lives" (Curtis, 1911, p.229). In fact, as Colarusso (1997) points out, so important are guests considered to be that

> In theory the host would even give his life to defend a guest. In return, the guest is expected to act discreetly and respectfully to his host and so bring honour to the host's family. Even a prisoner of war or an enemy could be treated hospitably if he had shown great valour. In the midst of a duel, it was possible for one adversary to seek a suspension of hostilities for a period of time as long as several days. The combatants would then resume their struggle at an agreed upon time and place.

And this is what Chenciner has to say on the way that the various peoples care for their guests:

> Once, every family in Daghestan had a lamp in their window in case a stranger needing help passed by in the night. When a guest entered a mountain house, he was first offered the sweet water from their spring. Nowadays he was also poured a strong drink ... If guests were from the host's village, he bade them goodbye at his gate. When they were from another village, he escorted them to the boundary of his village. If the guest was an important foreigner, he was accompanied to the frontier of the region, or even Daghestan, in a motorcade (Chenciner, 1997, pp.123-124).

As for living conditions, in the high reaches of Daghestan they can be extremely difficult due to the prolonged winters, coupled with the poor quality of the land. Men have to leave their families and go on long outings to earn money in the lowlands, and the women remain behind to maintain the households while they are away.

Another reason life was hard were the natural barriers to travel, with transport always having been a problem in the mountains, carved up as they are by torrential rivers. Most roads are nothing more than bulldozed rocks or dirt, full of pot-holes (see Chenciner,

1997, p.130).

One advantage to living in the highlands, though, is that it ensures plenty of exercise, which probably helps to explain why so many people live to such ripe old ages.

Survival often depended on there being an adequate harvest, which was at the mercy of the elements, and ceremonies in which offerings were made to invoke the rain evolved from human sacrifice to save crops in times of drought.

> In Karabudakent, after a prolonged drought, a meeting was announced from the minaret. Those with milk herds were asked to bring milk, and the rest to bring produce for the sacrificial meal. In a separate ceremony the women went up to their sacred place, while the men sacrificed a horned animal at the sacred well, dressed in skin coats turned inside out. They chanted a special prayer, shouting "Yes, we will have rain!" and then poured the water from the well over each other. Young men were made to jump into the cold water, after which they all went to the mosque for the meal (Chenciner, 1997, p.105).

Invocations for the sun were conducted along similar lines. "Girl mummers carried a doll-totem … from house to house, singing songs of supplication to the sun, for which they received presents (Chenciner, 1997, p.106).

The Northeast Caucasian stone houses generally run on top of one another, the roof of the lower serving as the porch of the upper, as they cling to hill sides to form compact villages called *auls.* Traditionally the houses tended to be built together "on a south-facing amphitheatre shaped slope for defence, light and warmth" (Chenciner, 1997, p.135). Made of local stone, the houses generally have two floors: the first for livestock, the second for people. One of the reasons for this arrangement is that in winter it enables the people to live above the snow.

There was something else that could be found in every home:

> Throughout the North Caucasus, every home possessed a wrought-iron hearth chain hanging down the chimney. Apart from the practical function of hooking up the cooking pot, the hearth chain has a central symbolic role for the family. … The chain represented a microcosmic link between the fire and the food, or prosperity of the family, and the heavens above, where the family ancestors lived. It was another variation of the universal cosmic pillar separating heaven and earth (Chenciner, 1997, p.151).

The verb "separating" should perhaps be replaced here with "linking" or "connecting", as that was the traditional use that the Tree of Life, the Sacred Mountain, or Jacob's Ladder were put to, enabling the shaman or equivalent figure to travel between the different worlds in order to serve the community he or she represented, and to act as an intermediary on their behalf.

"Since the collapse of the Soviet Union in 1991, Daghestan is virtually the only part of the Caucasus that has not suffered inter-ethnic conflicts. This is probably because there are no dominant ethnic minorities due to the topology and linked ethnic mosaic of the region. In addition, that is likely to be the reason for the richness of their arts" (Chenciner et al, 1997, p.9). Since 2000 however, the situation has changed in that Daghestan has been the venue of a low-level guerrilla war, bleeding over from Chechnya; the fighting has claimed the lives of hundreds of federal servicemen and officials – mostly members of local police forces – as well as many Daghestani national rebels and civilians.

There is a long history of conflict in the region prior to the Soviet era too, for Daghestan has "always been the prey of rival powers [and] … has been plundered and ravaged in turn by all the Asiatic hordes" (Curtis, 1911, pp.228-229).

> For millennia successive waves of conquerors have swept through the narrow coastal strip constricted at the 5,000-year-

> old city of Derbent. The road joins Russia and the Steppes to the north, Turkey to the west and Iran and the Middle East to the south. During the 6th century AD the Sassanian Persians built the double walls of Derbent up from the Caspian Sea to the mountains. After the Great Wall of China, the walls rank in size alongside Hadrian's Wall, or the triple walls of Constantinople (Chenciner et al, 1997, p.9).

It is said of the wall that it "extended from the present city of Derbent on the shore of the Caspian Sea, to the mountain of Koushan-Dagh near the western limits of Daghestan", and that "it was eighteen or twenty feet high and so thick that a squadron of cavalry could gallop along its top" (Curtis, 1911, p.233). And as for Derbent, it "was the conqueror's prize for Romans, Sarmatians, Sassanians, Georgians, Armenians, Khazars, Huns, Arabs, Mongols, Seljuk Turks, Ottoman Turks, Safavid Persians, Qajar Persians and Russians. It was not surprising that the ancient local tribes were great warriors. During the brief intervals of peace, they retreated to their independent mountain strongholds, to reunite again when faced with a fresh outside threat" (Chenciner et al, 1997, p.9).

As Colarusso (1997) points out, religious tolerance is a feature of the North Caucasus, where Sunni Muslims, Orthodox Christians, Jews, and pagans can all be found living amicably side by side, and this can probably be partly attributed to the fact that religion is socially and conceptually subordinated to ethnic identity throughout the region.

In the highlands there are mystical traditions of meditation and martial arts, which in Chechnya and Daghestan developed into Sufi practices. And in Daghestan holy men often have shrines, which are usually placed at the highest point of the village. Enigmatic relics of pagan beliefs persist throughout the Caucasus. In Daghestan, for example, there are many old beliefs surrounding animals, such as snakes, horses, and especially the bear.

On the subject of the early beliefs of the people, prior to the adoption of Islam, we also know that the cult of tree veneration was widespread, and sacred trees and groves are to be found in Daghestan, Ossetia and Ingushetia even today:

> In Daghestan, the ancestors believed that trees or groves were occupied by spirits. In their folktales there are several instances, for example, when a comb is thrown or drops out over the hero's shoulder, it changes into a tree or a branch that shields him or her from the force of evil. Another manifestation of the cult is that, until today, in the mountains, it is considered an irreparable sin to cut down a tree. In some villages there it is also customary to spread out head-scarves or rags on trees that grow in cemeteries. If there are no trees there, a pole is planted among the tombstones and it is dressed up as a substitute tree. As an echo of ancient sacrifice to the tree spirits, it is usual to 'plant' a false tree on which is hung the carcass of a ram, in front of a shepherd's wattle shelter. The dried tree branch is called *karats* (Chenciner et al, 1997, p.34).

We also know that when magical healing was called for,

> the Lezgin resorted to a witch doctor, who performed various rites. He collected earth from holy places or shrines, such as the Pyre of Suleiman on Mount Shalbuzdag, which was mixed with water and drunk as medicine. He also used the human-like Mary's hair, a fibrous plant which hangs from branches. If a prayer was said while a strand was tied round the wrist or ankle, magic powers of healing were activated (Chenciner, 1997, p.87).

In place of the term "witch doctor", with its negative connotations, it might be better to substitute "shaman" or even "medicine man" here, as their main role was one of healing too.

As for the negative side of curing, "The Lezgins in particular had discovered a most effective way to kill: by burying some of the victim's hairs, knotted with a woollen string and a fatty sheep's tail in a sunny place. As the fat melted, so the victim would sicken and die in torment" (Chenciner, 1997, p.87).

In addition to the Lezgin healers, "In Daghestan Sufi sheikhs and some elder-women tattooers appear to have similar roles to shamans in North Asia and elsewhere" (Chenciner et al, 1997, p.28). And because of their spiritual power, the North Caucasian Sufi sheikhs had a political role, as can be seen from the way in which they resisted the Tsarist Russians and then the Communists during the 19th and 20th centuries. However, as in the neighboring countries, the cult of the elders and ancestor worship play a more prominent role in the daily lives of the people, and the oral histories of shamans tend to be inconsistent individual stories rather than cultural models that have become generally adopted (see Chenciner et al, 1997, p.29).

***

The Avar people form one of the main linguistic groups of the Lezg people of Daghestan.

> The mountainous nature of the country and the bravery of their men has protected the Avars from external pressure except for the most persistent invaders. In the eighteenth century, the Avars were the only group in the area to successfully defy the Persian invasion of Nadir Shah. Shamyl, who fought a religious war so successfully for many years against the Russians in the last century, was also an Avar; as were also many of the greatest men of Daghestan. The Avars are generally devout Moslems ... and many of them make the pilgrimage to Mecca (Hunt, 2007, p.1).

However, this was clearly not always the case as the elements to be found in their folktales show, and as can be seen in the tale that follows:

***

Balai and Boti

Once upon a time there was a king who had three sons. But what we are about to relate happened after the death of the king.

The sons heard that there lived in the south a king who had a daughter: she had vowed she would marry no one but he who could overcome her in single combat. The eldest brother made up his mind to try his luck. He dressed himself in fine clothes, put on handsome weapons, mounted a good horse, and set out on his way after saying farewell to his brothers.

He rode on and on for a long way. He left broad valleys and deep gorges behind him, he crossed endless plains. And on his way he met an old man.

"Whither away, my son?" he asked; "where do you want to go, if God wills?" The young man told him all his plans.

"What is dearer to you," asked the old man, "the maiden or the counsel of old age?"

"I can give advice myself," answered the young man, "and the maiden is dearer to me than your counsels."

"Then, good journey to you, my son."

The young man rode on, and came at last to the town of the king whose daughter he had come to court. He dismounted before the great gate of the town; the king's men came at once and took his arms, led his horse away and showed him the guest-rooms. Then they set before him all that was best in the kitchen, brought him sweet wine to drink, and the vizier came to talk with him.

"Guest," said he, after they had eaten, drunk, and passed

some time in pleasant conversation, "Guest, what do you desire?"

"I desire to measure my strength against that of the king's daughter!"

"If that is truly your desire, know this: tomorrow morning at daybreak, be ready and go to the square. There you will find the princess. If fortune favours you, you will conquer her; but if she vanquishes you, your head will be cut off and stuck up on a pole." When he had thus spoken, the vizier got up and went away. These prospects did not make the guest particularly happy.

He could not get a wink of sleep the whole night through, but next morning he was punctually at his station. And as the sun rose out of the sea the princess arrived. Her armour shone brighter than the morning sun. She stepped forward, placed herself in front of her opponent and bared her breast. The young man swooned and fell down. Slaves hurried up, struck off his head and stuck it on a pole.

Some time passed, and then one day the second brother set out to enquire as to the fate of the eldest brother, and, if opportunity offered, to fight with the princess. He travelled by the same road, and met the same old man that the other brother had met. But why waste time telling all this? The adventure cost him also his head.

The youngest son waited long for the return of his brothers. Finally he made up his mind to go and see for himself what had happened to them. He also was determined to measure himself against the princess in single combat. He rode day and night till he met the old man.

"Whither away, my son?" he asked. "Where are you going, if God wills?"

The young man told him his intentions. "Which is dearer to you, the maiden or the advice of an old man?"

"The maiden does not displease me," answered the youth,

"but I should be glad to hear the advice of an old man."

"Hear, then!" returned the old man. "She does not conquer her adversaries by strength, but by opening her shift and baring her breast. Not even the strongest man can endure that. Therefore, if she tries the same method with you, cast your eyes down and rush at her; you will overpower her easily."

The youth thanked the old man for his advice, urged his horse forward, and rode on. When he came to the gate of the king's town he dismounted. And just as had happened to his brothers, the king's servants helped him, fed him and gave him wine to drink, and the vizier came and entertained him ... in fact, everything happened just as it had done to the two elder brothers.

Before sunrise the youth rose, and with the sun the princess arrived. She opened her shift and bared her breast, but the youth did not let his eyes rest on her, he rushed at her instead and overcame her. "Shall I spare you, you wretch, or shall I cut off your head?" he demanded, holding his dagger at her throat. "Spare me! I am yours!" besought the vanquished princess. "Then come away with me at once," he replied, "I must get home quickly."

"I will come," said the princess, "if you will do one thing for me. Otherwise I will not come with you and will not marry you."

"If you had conquered me," the youth replied, "my head would by now have been stuck on a pole – and yet you even demand services from me! So be it. You are a woman. I could not descend to trickery as you do. Command me! What must I do?" Then the princess took a golden slipper out of a box and threw it down before the youth. "The neighbour to that is lost," she said. "Find it!"

He stuck the slipper in his knapsack, mounted his horse and rode away. He rode fast, he rode slow, he crossed high mountains and deep gorges, he crossed broad rivers, he rode over endless plains till he came to a beautiful meadow covered with flowers. In the middle of the meadow there was a garden as lovely as Paradise, and in the garden beautiful tents were erected. He dismounted by the tents, let his horse loose and went in. Everything was in order, but no living soul was within. In the centre of the tent a spring bubbled up. He bathed in it, and then lay down to sleep. After a time someone wakened him.

"Well, friend," said the new-comer, "is this perhaps the garden of your father, that you let your horse loose in it? Get up and show your courage!" Our hero sprang up, looked round him and saw a youth with a beaming countenance. "How will you fight, on foot or on horseback?" the youth asked him. "On foot," came the answer. They closed with each other and fought and fought, but neither of them could throw the other. They wrestled on … till midday, till afternoon – the sun was about to sink, and still they both stood upright. "Enough!" said the unknown, "let me go. Tomorrow morning early I will come again. My sheep are pasturing behind that hill, go there this evening and eat and drink, for no one will come to wait on you here." Having so spoken, he disappeared.

Our hero rode over to where the sheep were grazing. The shepherds came to meet him, held his horse, took off his cloak, killed a sheep, put the roasting spit on the fire, and showed him every hospitality. When he had eaten and drunk, the shepherds went away; only he and one young man were left sitting by the fire. "Whom do these sheep belong to?" asked our hero. "They all belong to a maiden whose castle is not far from here, and the castle is guarded by two dragons."

After our hero had enquired the way to the castle, he took a carcase of mutton with him and rode towards it. He opened the gate and rode in, when two dragons rushed towards him. He tore the sheep in two and threw a half to each of them. Then he pushed on into the building, and came to the young man with whom he had wrestled, lying fast asleep. It was not a young man, however, but a maiden. "Stand up, wretch," said our hero and laid his hand on her breast, "I will rather fight with you by night than by day!" The maiden sprang up at once, they closed with each other, and they fought and they wrestled, but neither could get the other down.

When every other means had failed him, our hero pressed the maiden's right breast – something cracked like a nut – and the maiden fell down. "Now I am yours, you can do with me what you will," she said. And she had no sooner spoken than a mullah came out of one corner, his budun out of the other, and they celebrated the marriage of the two. Now they were man and wife [A mullah is a Muslim priest and a budun is his assistant].

They stayed together for three nights: on the fourth night our hero made himself ready to depart. "Whither away, what is your hurry?" asked his wife. "Where did you come from?" Then he told her what had happened between him and the king's daughter, pulled the slipper out of his knapsack and threw it down before her. "But this slipper must have fallen off my foot," said his wife. "Where else could she have got it?" And she gave him the other one.

Our hero puts both slippers in his knapsack, bade his wife farewell, swung himself up on his horse, and rode away.

When he got back to the king's daughter, he threw her the slippers, saying, "There you are, take them!" "Very good!" said she. "But there is a man called Balai who has a wife called Boti. If you do not discover for me what has passed between them, then I will not marry you." Our hero only shook his head, mounted again and rode off by a way which no one had ever ridden before. He rode fast, he rode slow, he rode day and night, he rode a long, long, endless way till at last he came to a land in which there was mud when the sun shone and dust when it rained. He dismounted and fastened his horse under a tree whose branches lost themselves in heaven. He looked round, he looked up, and at last he saw at the very top of the tree an eagle's nest with young eagles in it, each one as big as an ox. He climbed up and a three-headed dragon followed on his heels – but with one stroke our hero cut off all three heads. In a short time the mother eagle flew up – trees and mountains swayed with her flight – and sat down on her nest. "Welcome, hero!" the mother eagle called out to him, "let me be your mother now, and you my son! You have destroyed the enemy of my children. Ask what you will! However great your wish may be, I will fulfil it."

"Carry me to Balai's and Boti's house," said our hero. "If you wish to do me a service, that is what I want most."

"Ah! But if we go there, neither of us will ever return!" said the mother eagle. "Ask something else. You can stay here while I carry out your commands."

"I have nothing else to ask you," answered our hero, "if you will not come with me yourself, at least show me the way there."

"No, if you will go to certain death, then I may not stay behind," replied the mother eagle. "Seat yourself on my back."

And she spread her wings; with every flap of her wings another mountain was left behind, or a river or a country; at last she glided down on to the peak of a high hill. Before the hill stood a tower which seemed to stretch up to heaven.

"Balai and Boti live in this tower," said the mother eagle, "go to them, say what you have to say, ask what you have to ask, and come back here in due time. If you have good fortune, he will not let his arrow fly at you till you have reached me; if you have not good fortune … well, no one has ever come back from them before you, and no one will ever come back after you." Our hero went to the tower.

"Will you receive a guest?" he asked.

"Why not, friend?" answered Balai, who stood up, took him by the hand, asked him to come in and sit down, and enquired where he came from and what he wanted. Our hero told him everything down to the smallest detail.

"Well, well, we will have something to eat first," declared Balai, "and then I will tell you what passed between Boti and myself." The food was brought; when they had finished, Balai gave what was over to a greyhound, and what was left after that to a woman who was already half turned to stone and stood behind the door. She did not want to eat; Balai took up a whip and threatened her with it – and she ate. Our hero lost patience with him and asked why he gave the woman what the dog had left, and what her sin had been.

"I am Balai," said the master of the house, "and that is my wife. After we married we lived for a long time in perfect concord. But then, whenever I lay down beside her, she became cold, as cold as a heap of snow, as cold as an icicle. (When he goes away – said Balai to himself – I will shoot the arrow after him.) I came to be suspicious of her, and watched her secretly. One night I made a cut in my thumb and put salt in the wound that I might not go to sleep, and lay down beside her pretending to be asleep. (As soon as he goes I will let the arrow fly after him) . . . After a time I saw how she got up, dressed herself and left the house. I got up too, took my weapons and followed her. I had two horses in the stable, one of the winds, the other of the clouds. She took out the horse of the winds and mounted it, I did the same with the horse of the clouds, and rode after her. (Whenever he goes I will shoot the arrow after him.) She in front, I after her; she in front, I after her. But the horse of the winds was swifter than the horse of the clouds; I did not lose sight of her certainly, but I fell behind. We rode for some time like this till we came to the tower of the Narts. Boti tied up her horse at the foot, and climbed up to the top storey; I did the same. (Whenever he goes I will shoot the arrow after him.) She opened a door and went in; I stood so that she could not see me and watched her. There were seven Nart brothers inside who amused themselves by throwing my wife from one to another, as children play with a ball. When they were tired of that game they began to eat and drink. And when they tired of that too, one of the brothers came outside; with one stroke of my sword I struck his head off, and that I repeated with five more of them. (Whenever he goes I will shoot the arrow after him.) There only remained my wife and the youngest Nart in the room. 'I will surely get the better of one,' I thought to myself, and went in. But the youngest drew his sword and set upon me. Boti ran to the side and watched us. I struck, he struck; I don't know whether I had more luck or more skill, anyway I struck off one of his legs. He fell to the ground, and Boti ran out of the room. (Whenever he goes I will send an arrow after him.) I left the Nart lying there and ran after my wife, but before I could catch her she had mounted the horse of the winds and ridden off. I sprang on my horse of the clouds and made after her. She got home before me, took my magic whip in her hand, and waited for me; I was hardly into the room before she struck me with it, and said, 'Change into a dog,' and I became a dog. (Whenever he goes I will send an arrow after him.) For seven years I remained a shepherd's dog; in the eighth year she struck me again with the magic whip and I changed into a hawk. I flew straight home. After a short time Boti came too, she hung the whip on a nail and went out. I flew to the whip, struck against it, and said, 'Change me back into Balai as I was before!' And it was so. (Whenever he goes I will shoot an arrow after him..) I took the whip and flung myself on my wife; she started back, gave a dreadful cry, and fell to the ground. 'Do not be afraid,' I said to her, 'I will not kill you, but you must suffer what I have had to suffer. Change into a sheep-dog.' And as long as I had herded sheep so she had now to herd them. Then I changed her into a mule, then into a being half human and half stone as she is now, and she gets the scraps left by the dogs for her food. (Whenever he goes I will shoot an arrow after him.) And now know this: the king's daughter who overcame your brothers is a sister of Boti's. And the Nart whose leg I struck off is really her husband. She hides him in a cellar under the room in which she lives, and she has a son by him. Now you know what passed between Balai and Boti; but … (Whenever he goes I will shoot an arrow after him.)"

When Balai had finished speaking, our hero said: "May I look over your house and court now?" He went out, and ran as fast as he could to where the mother eagle awaited him. She took him at once on her back and carried him away with great sweeps of her mighty wings. She left high mountains and deep ravines behind her: she flew as on the wings of the storm.

But Balai waited and waited for his guest, who was looking over his house and court, as Balai thought. He waited for a long time, he waited till midday … but the guest did not return. "What can have happened to him?" said Balai and went out to look for him. All in vain. When at last dawned on Balai that his guest had made good his escape, he shot an arrow after him which struck the eagle on one of her wings. Feathers flew all about as if out of a torn cushion. "Has he hit you?" the eagle asked our hero. "No, the arrow flew past under my left ear," he answered, "and cut off some of my hair: how are you?" "My bones are not touched," said the mother eagle, "if we have any luck, he won't shoot again." Balai did not shoot again and the eagle carried our hero back to the king's town and then flew home to her own nest.

But our hero called all the inhabitants of the town together – the king, the vizier, and all the people – and led them to the princess. There he related all that he had learnt from Balai. The princess was embarrassed, but denied everything. "That is not true," she said; "you have not even seen Balai, for no one can escape his arrow. How did you escape his shot?"

"If you wish to know which of us is lying," said our hero to the king, "then look in the cellar under your daughter's room. For the man whose leg Balai struck off must be there. He is now the lame husband of your daughter; and her son must be there too. If I have lied, then you may kill me, but if I have spoken the truth, put this miserable wretch to death." The princess got deadly pale at these words. But that availed her nothing; the search was made, and what our hero had said was found to be true. "You have brought shame and disgrace on my head," said the king and struck down his daughter; while our hero gave the finishing stroke to the Nart and his son.

After all these deeds and after he had come through so many dangers unharmed, our hero went back to his wife and became king in his own country (taken from Dirr. A. (1925) *Caucasian Folk-tales,* translated into English by Lucy Menzies, London & Toronto: J.M. Dent & Sons Ltd.).

***

Once again, as in so many tales from the Caucasus, the numbers three and seven feature prominently. The king has three sons, after marrying the princess the youngest son stays with her for three days, and then he overcomes a three-headed dragon. And as for the number seven, there are seven Nart brothers and Balai has to live as a shepherd dog for seven years.

We know the ancients believed there were seven planets in total and it is possible that over the course of time these were transformed into seven deities. The Egyptians had seven higher gods; the Phœnicians seven kabiris; the Persians, seven sacred horses of Mithra; the Parsees, seven angels opposed by seven demons, and seven celestial abodes with seven lower regions too.

For the Egyptians there were seven states of purification and progressive perfection in the process of the transmigration of the soul, and for the Buddhists seven stages of progressive development of the disembodied soul. Additionally, in the worship of Mithra there were "seven gates," seven altars, and seven mysteries. The supposed seven planets even served as a model for state divisions and organizations, with China being divided into seven provinces and ancient Persia into seven satrapies. The number seven also played an important part in the architecture of temples and palaces. For example, the famous Cathedral of Cologne, which displays this number even in the smallest architectural details. This applied to cities too, with Rome being built on seven hills and Istanbul being called the city on the seven hills.

The Romans divided the week into seven days, with the seventh being regarded as the most sacred (the Sol of Jupiter), and the Pythagoreans considered the figure seven the image and model of the divine order and harmony in nature. There are also seven notes in a musical scale. The ancients divided the human frame into seven parts; the head, the chest, the stomach, two hands and two feet; and man's life was divided into seven ages too.

A lot of what is written about the number seven is clearly a load of nonsense, though. Take the following quote, for example, from an article by H. P. Blavatsky entitled 'The Number Seven' in *Theosophist*, June, 1880.

> A baby begins teething in the seventh month; a child begins to sit after fourteen months (2 X 7); begins to walk after twenty-one months (3 X 7); to speak after twenty-eight months (4 X 7); leaves off sucking after thirty-five months (5 X 7); at fourteen years (2 X 7) he begins to finally form himself; at twenty-one (3 X 7) he ceases growing.

As we all know only too well from personal experience, apart from what educational psychologists have to say on the subject, it is impossible to generalize in this manner and there is no such hard and fast rule. So although the number has clearly been included in the story intentionally and for a reason, it would at the same time be dangerous to read too much into its significance and to thus fall into the same trap that Blavatsky and others have. What we can say, however, is that through the inclusion of the number, as a result of the associations it carries, the story is given more substance and it thus has a more powerful impact than it would otherwise have had.

As is so often the case in stories that feature three sons, it is the youngest who proves himself to be the most worthy, and the old man he meets along the way plays the role of his spirit helper.

Of the princess we learn that "Her armour shone brighter than the morning sun." Associating beauty with the sun is often found in stories from the Caucasus, and is undoubtedly a reference to the time when sun worship was widespread in the region, partly as a result of the influence of Zoroastrianism and partly the result of local pagan beliefs and practices.

As we might expect from a people who live what is, to a large extent, "a relatively communal life, but who suffered oppression in the past, either from outsiders or from their own petty princes, many of the tales are an attempt to 'hit back' at authority" (Hunt, 2007, p.4). And by exposing the true circumstances of the princess who has spent more or less the entire tale taking advantage of him at the conclusion, our hero succeeds in doing precisely this.

> Travellers to Daghestan have generally commented on the hard life lived by women. During courting, of course, there was a display of feelings of tenderness by the man. Various complimentary descriptions would be made ... After marriage, however, a woman had to work very hard, and generally the older she was the harder she worked, particularly if she became a widow ... Another universal chore for women was the collection of water from the well or spring ... Since the terrain tends to be mountainous and water usually occurs at a low level, this usually meant carrying the full jars uphill. ... In spite of this hard work, it was a woman's ideal to be married ...an Avar proverb: "Light is the grave of a widow without a husband; the sky is the grave slab of a girl without a lover" ...The relations between young men and girls before marriage is strongly governed by the need to preserve the girl's chastity. The normal

> procedure is for the suitor to send matchmakers to make arrangements with the girl's father (Hunt, 2007, p.2).

The early representations of women in Daghestan however, such as a seventh century B.C. figure that was found in the village of Sogratl, of a naked female charioteer, holding the reins, "show evidence of matriarchal (or at least equal) societies" (Chenciner, 1997, p40) and suggest that Daghestan "was a possible homeland for the legendary Amazons of classical antiquity" (Chenciner, 1997, p.40). And the tradition of strong women still survives. Daghestan women fought the Russians, both under Shamil and during the Revolution, and today, at work in the villages, they can be seen carrying up to double their own weight on their backs (see Chenciner, 1997, p.41).

The manner in which the princess in our story clearly wears the trousers in her relationship with our hero harks back to the time of just such a matriarchal society, and is also an indication of the great age of the tale.

In "a garden as lovely as Paradise" our hero bathes in a bubbling spring and then falls into a dream or a trance state. The waters have been described as the reservoir of all the potentialities of existence because they not only precede every form but they also serve to sustain every creation. Immersion is equivalent to dissolution of form, in other words death, whereas emergence repeats the cosmogenic act of formal manifestation, in other words re-birth (see Eliade, 1991, p.151).

Spring waters, as well as herbs and spells, also form an integral part of folk medicine in Daghestan:

> Spring waters, herbs and spells form an integral part of this medicine ... The curing spring beside the waterfall at Inkhokvari, near Aguali village is one such mysterious example. When the moon waxes, there is more gas in the pungent waters, when the moon wanes, less, and the flavour changes. Here I met

> ailing Jakhfar Gazi Magomedov, whose sons had brought him 200 kilometres to cure his stomach by drinking the waters. They then prayed on mats by the river. Earlier this century, on the night of the equinox, even ordinary spring water was considered to have medicinal properties by the Kumyks, who either bathed in the river or brought home ewers filled with its water to pour over themselves and their elderly relatives. They used special brass bowls, with central raised bosses and magical inscriptions, for drinking remedial waters (Chenciner, 1997, p.85).

Water plays an important part in a number of rituals the Mountain Jews practise in Daghestan too. On Rash ha-Shanah, for example (which, for the majority of Jews, marks the beginning of the New Year) the Mountain Jews observe the *tashlikh* ceremony. This involves people saying prayers near a source of water so as to "cast" their sins into it. There is also an old Caucasian Jewish practice that entails expelling bad dreams by "telling them to the river" (see Mikdash-Shamailov, 2002, p.81).

The introduction by the princess of the golden slipper and the request made to the youngest son to find its missing partner suggests that the story of Cinderella was not unfamiliar to the storyteller, and the castle "guarded by two dragons" represents the barrier between the two worlds our hero is required to pass through in order to accomplish his mission.

The fact that their marriage is conducted by a mullah does not detract from the pagan origins of the tale for it should be remembered that in Daghestan, as is generally the case in the Caucasus, pagan rituals have been, and are still, practised by the people whatever religion they may profess to belong to.

The Caucasus is rich in folklore and this includes the Nart sagas, dramatic tales of a race of ancient heroes, who make an appearance in this tale too. The Nart giants originally featured in the Ossetic epic poems, and then spread south to Daghestan as characters in folktales and anecdotes. As is usually the case, they total seven in number, and the significance of the number has already been commented on earlier in this work.

That the princess should defeat her suitors by exposing her breast should come as no surprise as

> Ritual sucking at the breast of the head female of a family is a well-known procedure in the Caucasus for the adoption of a person into the family [and certainly pre-dates the conversion of the people to Islam]. Her natural sons thereby become the foster brothers of the newly-adopted son (Hunt, 2007, p.5).

As Colarusso (1997) points out, this was also one of the traditional ways of putting an end to a blood feud: The killer "would sneak up on a woman from the victim's clan, seize her, tear open her blouse, and place his lips to her breast. Such an act, however fleeting, would suffice to create a kinship bond between the two clans which precluded further bloodshed".

> In the last century, when a son was born to the ruler of the Karakaitags, he was sent from village to village to be suckled by all the women who could, in order to make him foster-brother of his entire generation. This was often a stronger tie than blood; Steder, a traveller-scholar of German origin, writing in 1797 noted that an Ingush murderer suckled his victim's mother at knifepoint, and so became part of her family, to avoid death by the blood-feud. Not long later, the Russian Karginov heard of an Ossete adulterer, who had been forced to kiss the breast of his beloved by her family, to terminate their relationship by making it incestuous (Chenciner, 1997, p.81).

To find out what has passed between Balai and Boti a horse is our hero's chosen form of transport. "The *djigit* was a dare-devil mounted warrior, whose sure-footed horse could float over the terrain, scattered with loose protruding rocks, punctuated with fast deep rivulets and sudden ravines" (Chenciner, 1997, p.20), and this is what our hero is clearly intended to be an example of.

For Balai and Boti's journey into non-ordinary reality that takes them to the tower of the Narts, they employ horses too, the horse of the winds and the horse of the clouds. And as has already been commented upon, the horse is also frequently the form of transport used by shamans to access other worlds.

> Pre-eminently the funerary animal and psychopomp, the "horse" is employed by the shaman, in various contexts, as a means of achieving ecstasy, that is, the "coming out of oneself" that makes the mystical journey possible. This mystical journey – to repeat – is not necessarily in the infernal direction. The "horse" enables the shaman to fly through the air, to reach the heavens. The dominant aspect of the mythology of the horse is not infernal but funerary; the horse is a mythical image of death and hence is incorporated into the ideologies and techniques of ecstasy. The horse carries the deceased into the beyond; it produces the "break-through in plane," the passage from this world to other worlds (Eliade, 1964, p.467).

However, the infernal direction, contrary to what Eliade suggests, is not necessarily to the Lower World, just as Heaven is not necessarily only found in the sky.

In order to discover what has passed between Balai and Boti, we learn of the youngest son that "He rode fast, he rode slow, he rode day and night, he rode a long, long, endless way till at last he came to a land in which there was mud when the sun shone and dust when it rained. He fastened his horse under a tree whose branches lost themselves in heaven." The implications are clear; that he has entered another reality, the land of the Narts, where the rules of our reality no longer apply, where a three-headed dragon can be found, for example, and then be destroyed with just one blow.

Let us now consider the significance of the hero's encounter with the eagle in our tale. "A shaman is a man who has immediate, concrete experiences with gods and spirits; he sees them face to face, he talks with them, prays to them, implores them-but he does not "control" more than a limited number of them" (Eliade, 1989, p.88). Most of these helpers have animal forms and the eagle clearly represents one in the story as he serves the purpose of helping our hero to succeed in his mission. However, the fact that thc helper is an eagle rather than any other animal is important too as the following Buryat tale about the origin of shamans suggests:

> In the beginning there were only the gods (*tengri*) in the west and evil spirits in the east. The gods created man, and he lived happily until the time came when the evil spirits spread sickness and death over the earth. The gods decided to give mankind a shaman to combat disease and death, and they sent the eagle. But men did not understand its language; besides, they had no confidence in a mere bird. The eagle returned to the gods and asked them to give him the gift of speech, or else to send a Buryat shaman to men. The gods sent him back with an order to grant the gift of shamanizing to the first person he should meet on earth. Returned to earth, the eagle saw a woman asleep under a tree, and had intercourse with her. Some time later the woman gave birth to a son, who became the "first shaman." According to another variant, the woman, after her connection with the eagle, saw spirits and herself became a shamaness (Eliade, 1989, p.69).

For this reason, the appearance of an eagle in a vision is often interpreted as a sign of shamanic vocation. This is not only the case in Siberian myths but can be found in the Native American tradition too,

The three-headed dragon is most probably a reference to Azhi

Dahaka, a demonic figure in the texts and mythology of Zoroastrianism, where he is described as a three-headed, dragon-like monster. He is said to have a thousand senses, and to bleed snakes, scorpions, and other venomous creatures. He also is said to bring or control storms and disease. This dragon was defeated by the hero Thraetaona, but could not be killed; instead, he was imprisoned by being chained to the mountain Damavand, the highest peak in Iran, there to remain until the end of the world.

All over the world shamans are credited with power to fly and this magical power, by all accounts, is often the result of their having been exposed to a ritual ascent during a period of apprenticeship, or of their having had an ecstatic experience or a vision that announced their shamanic vocation. And this is what our hero can be said to have had in this tale.

The symbolism of the eagle was already clearly established in the ancient Mesopotamian epic of Etana, which begins with an eagle and a serpent swearing an oath of friendship to each other before Shamash, the god of the sun. The eagle lives in the top of a tree and the serpent at its base, and for a time they and their young share every kill. One day the eagle eats the young of the serpent, who then burrow in the carcass of a bull. As soon as the eagle approaches to eat, the serpent bites it, cuts its wings, and throws the bird into a pit to die of hunger and thirst. Shamash sends the hero Etana to rescue and nurse the eagle and it becomes his guide. Etana then flies up to the heavens on the back of the eagle to ask Ishtar, a goddess of fertility, for the plant of birth so he can have a son, and this leads to the founding of the first Sumerian dynasty.

Some say the first shaman was in fact born from the union between an eagle and a woman, and the shaman can thus be regarded as a bird in the sense that, like the bird, he/she has access to the higher regions when he/she journeys to the Upper World (see Eliade,1989, pp.159-160).

The motif of a tree with an eagle at the top and a hostile serpent at the base has often been found in myth and legend, and another example is the three-rooted ash Yggdrasil, the Norse tree of life:

> One [root] spreads out towards the upper spring, *Urdur*, where the Ases hold council and where the Nornes, whilst settling the duration of the lives of men, pour water from the spring over the Tree in order to secure for it an endless sap and verdure. The second root stretches towards the land of the giants of the Frost; under this root springs the well of Mimir the first man and king of the dead; in this well all knowledge and all wisdom dwell; Odin himself, in order to quench his thirst with its waters, had to leave one of his eyes in pledge. As for the third, it descends to Nifleim, the Scandinavian Hades, where it is ever gnawed at by a dragon. On the highest bough of the stem an eagle perches whilst other animals occupy the lower branches (D'Alviella, 1894, p.167).

There are parallels to be found in myths and legends from other cultures too:

> The Goldi, the Dolgan, and the Tungus say that, before birth, the souls of children perch like little birds on the branches of the Cosmic Tree and the shamans go there to find them. This mythical motif ... is not confined to Central and North Asia; it is attested, for example, in Africa and Indonesia. The cosmological schema Tree-Bird (= Eagle), or Tree with a Bird at its top and a Snake at its roots, although typical of the peoples of Central Asia and the ancient Germans, is presumably of Oriental origin, but the same symbolism is already formulated on pre-historic monuments. In cultures where the unborn perch as birds in the World Tree, the initiate journeys there in spirit because he, too,

is going to undergo a new birth (Eliade, 1989, p.272-273).

The baby eagles in the nest in our story are like the souls of children in the Cosmic Tree referred to above, and our hero plays the role of the shaman as he climbs up the tree to save them.

As for the eagle and the Caucasus, Zeus the god of thunder sent an eagle to peck at the liver of the disobedient titan Prometheus each day, as he lay chained to a rock in the Caucasus Mountains. The liver would grow back during the night, and the cycle continued until the eagle was finally slain with an arrow shot by Hercules.

The ability to shape-shift, as Balai and Boti do, is of course one of the attributes traditionally associated with shamans.

Shape-shifting can be viewed as the imitation of the actions and voices of animals, though shamans themselves would certainly not describe what they do in such terms. During his/her apprenticeship, the future shaman has to learn the secret language that is required to communicate with the animal spirits and how to take possession of them, and this is often the "animal language" itself or a form of language derived from animal cries. It is regarded as equivalent to knowing the secrets of nature and hence evidence of the ability to prophesy.

By sharing in the animal mode of being, the shaman can be seen to be re-establishing the situation that existed in mythical times, when man and animal were one (see Eliade, 1989, pp.96-98).

There are many accounts of the incredible feats supposedly performed by shamans. For example, it was said of the Lapp shamans, the *noiaidi*, that as well as having the power to summon herds of wild reindeer, they were also able to transform themselves into animal forms – such as a wolf, a bear, a reindeer, or a fish (see Ripinsky-Naxon, 1993, p.63).

According to Philip "Greywolf" Shallcrass, described as a Druid shaman, shape-shifters, also known as "theriomorphs", can be found in both the Irish and the Welsh traditions too. *Fintan mac*

Bochra, for example, regarded as a fount of wisdom by the Irish *filidh,* transforms into an eagle, a salmon and a stag. And in the Welsh *Mabinogion, Lleu Llaw Gyffes* transforms into an eagle, while other characters become deer or wolves. Then there is the Story of Taliesin, which has the bard and the goddess Ceridwen both going through a series of animal transformations (cited in Wallis, 2003, pp.86-87).

The belief in a human's ability to change into an animal form also flourished in Renaissance Italy. Among the authors of the many learned and respected books that were published on the subject was one by a friend and colleague of Galileo, Giovanni Batista Porta. His book *Naturall Magick* described the process of metamorphosis by the use of psychotropic substances (see Ripinsky-Naxon, 1993, pp.63-64).

As in the case of voodoo, shape-shifting can be seen as a way of shifting responsibility away from the self and externalizing evil – the animal is seen as responsible for perpetrating the crime, not the "shaman" who shape-shifts into that form.

Through shape-shifting shamans can be said to be "identifying themselves with the very powers that deeply threaten them, and …enhancing their own powers by the very power that threatens to enfeeble them" (Turner, 1995, p.174) and this parallels what children unconsciously do when they play games.

The earliest example of a human taking on an animal role in Daghestan

is from a 14th-century worn carved stone relief from Koubachi village, which appears to portray a man, rushing on clawed bird-like feet, wearing a *simurgh*-bird head mask with long feathers streaming behind. The wavy serpent coiled in submission around his waist reproduces the other partner in this Zoroastrian cosmic conflict. This was the religion of the Sassanians, whose Iranian emperor, Khosrows, built the walls of Derbent, just a day's ride from Koubachi, down to the

Caspian sea (Chenciner, 1997, p.196).

Shape-shifting can still be seen to be taking place, even in our own times, in the way shamans have evolved and survived into the 21st century by developing preservation strategies. This has enabled them to adapt to the new situations they find themselves in and so remain relevant to the communities they serve.

All ritual sequences can be seen to arise out of some condition of social disunity, actual or potential, and such disunity can often provide the starting point to folktales too. The social disunity in this particular case has its starting point in the fact that the king is dead and no successor to him seems to have been chosen. By the end of the tale, though, the condition of social disunity has been resolved as a result of the hero's actions, with the aid of the spirit helpers he meets in the course of his journey.

Within indigenous communities, however, unlike what takes place in neo-shamanic circles, ritual is "pre-eminently concerned with the health of the corporate body, with securing balance and harmony between its parts ... rather than [with] individual men and women" (Turner, 1981, p.270) and this could well result in individuals being required to subordinate their individuality to their responsibilities to the community. In other words, the shaman is primarily concerned with the modal state of the community. For example, as Hoskins points out in the case of the Kodi, the ultimate goal of the rite is to repair social relations and "heal the group" (see Hoskins, 1996, pp.287-288). In neo-shamanic circles, on the other hand, the reality is that there is no such sense of there being a corporate body of people who live and work together on a daily basis, which clearly impacts on the form neo-shamanic rituals take.

Neo-shamanism (also known as "modern shamanism", "new shamanism", "urban shamanism" and "contemporary shamanism") can be said to be a mix of shamanic traditions taken from different cultures, blended into a new complex of beliefs and practices. Rowena Pattee (Kryder) PhD, a popular writer on neo-shamanism and workshop leader, defines a neo-shaman as "a modern person whose experiences of dying to the limited self and of the resultant ecstasy lead to self-empowerment and sacrifice for the benefit of his or her community" (Pattee, 1988, p.17). However, whether the techniques learnt are necessarily used to benefit the community is open to question as many take up the practices purely for personal development.

Chapter 8

Conclusions

There is an old saying which goes "This is my grandfather's axe. My father gave it a new helve, and I gave it a new head", and this very much applies, as we have seen, to the way in which religious beliefs and practices have evolved in the region. For what we have found on this journey through the Caucasus is that despite the establishment of Orthodox Christian, Moslem and Jewish faiths in the region, pagan practices are still widespread. To give but one of many examples, offerings to invoke rain or the sun have long been made in the region, and rituals to bring about rain are still conducted in Daghestan today even though the majority of the people who practise them would no doubt describe themselves as Moslems:

> In Karabudakent, after a prolonged drought, a meeting was announced from the minaret. Those with milk herds were asked to bring milk, and the rest to bring produce for the sacrificial meal. In a separate ceremony the women went up to their sacred place, while the men sacrificed a horned animal at the sacred well, dressed in skin coats turned inside out. They chanted a special prayer, shouting "Yes, we will have rain!" and then poured the water from the well over each other. Young men were made to jump into the cold water, after which they all went to the mosque for a meal.
>
> Until the 1900s, all over Daghestan, the mullah presented his village with a sheep's shoulder bone with Arabic inscriptions to encourage rain. In Khurik, the inhabitants gathered in their holy place, and after the sacrificial meal, they ran to the river and poured water over each other. The Lak had a variety of

> scapegoat totems: straw-doll, straw-cat or straw-donkey. The Avar poet, Rasul Gamzatov wrote that when the earth cracked in the heat, trees drooped, and fields dried up and plants, birds, sheep and people longed together for heavenly water (his Tsada) villagers picked a boy as a rain-donkey. Dressed up in coloured cloths, like grass faded by the sun, he was led on a rope through the village by children, chanting to Allah for rain. The women of the village ran out after the rain donkey, with jugs or basins and poured water over him, while the children responded "Amen, amen!" (Chenciner, 1997, p.105).

Similarly, despite the fact most Georgians would describe themselves as Orthodox Christians, folk customs with pagan origins, such as the use of songs in rituals for healing purposes that are chanted over sick children, are still practised alongside Christianity in the mountainous regions of the country.

The *bat'onebi*, for example, are spirits who are believed to live beyond the Black Sea and they are sent out by their superior in all directions, in order to test the loyalty of mankind. During the daytime, the *bat'onebi* move about on mules. In the evening, however, they return to the houses of the sick and reside in the bodies of the stricken. *Bat'onebi* are to be obeyed without question, as resistance only enrages them. Nonetheless, their hearts can be conquered with tenderness and caresses; thus, it is possible to protect oneself from calamity. They are said to enjoy gentle songs and the bright sound of instrumental music.

The blisters from chickenpox (*qvavili,* literally: flowers) and the redness from measles (*ts'itela,* literally: redness) are said to be signs of the arrival of the *bat'onebi*. In preparation for the ritual, the patient's bed and room are decorated with colorful fabrics and flowers. Visitors wear red or white garments and walk around the sick person with presents for the *bat'onebi* in their hands. A table full of sweets and a kind of Christmas tree are prepared for them too. If the illness becomes worse, the family of the patient turn to the ritual of "asking-for-pardon" (*sabodisho*) and a *mebodishe,* a woman who has access to the *bat'onebi* and acts as a mediator, is invited to contact them to find out what they want and to win them over. Once the patient recovers, the *bat'onebi* have to be escorted on their way, back to where they came from.

The following description of a ritual observed by the Canadian anthropologist Kevin Tuite provides a further example of the pagan practices that are still prevalent in the country:

> As the hot lamb's blood congealed on her hands, a young woman responded to the questions of a curious visitor. We were standing on the banks of the St'ekura, in the northeast Georgian province of Xevsureti, in the one part of the territory of Xaxmat'i's Jvari not off-limits to females. Not even a hundred kilometres as the crow flies from Tbilisi, we were in a part of Georgia very few Georgians, even now, ever visit; without electricity or all-season roads, it remains an eerily archaic outpost on the remote periphery of Europe. On a chilly July morning, the woman had come to Xevsureti's most sacred shrine, lamb in tow, to undergo the cleansing ritual known as *ganatvla.* She knelt before the priest (*xucesi*) as he intoned a prayer of benediction and healing, invoking St. George, his female partner Samdzimari, and a host of saints, angels and "children of God" (*xvtisšvilni*). He extracted his dagger, and slit the lamb's throat. Its blood spilled forth onto the woman's arms, coating them up to the elbow. Following the ancient principle that the good blood of a slaughtered animal drives out the bad blood of female impurity, she hoped that the sacrifice would free her of certain "impediments" (*dabrk'olebebi*) in her life's course. She saw no contradiction between this ritual and the canons of the Orthodox church; both were integral parts of her Christian faith, both marked her as a Georgian and as a believer (*morc'mune*) (Tuite, 2004, pp.1-2).

Although there is no mention of hereditary shamans as such in the history of Georgian paganism, the *khevisberi* in the northeast Georgian highlands would seem to have fulfilled a similar role. It was

> the *khevisberi*, far more than any distant priest or power, who directed the spiritual, ritual and moral affairs of the mountains. He was and is elected by his peers, not on the basis of age or wealth, but for his deeper qualities [specialized ritual, mythological, and esoteric knowledge inherited from his ancestors]. Sometimes his office is given to him in dreams. He decides on all questions of law, presides over festivals and sacred ceremonies; he, alone, approaches the shrine and undertakes the sacrifice and in so doing brings peace to the dead and placates the deities (Anderson, 2003, p.144).

As for the shrine, the sacred space where ceremonies are performed, it is known as the *khati*. It is the place

> where people gather to make offerings, to eat and drink and sacrifice and also to dance and sing ritual, improvised songs, the *kaphiaoba*. The word *khati* has other significant religious and spiritual meanings [too]: it is the name given to the Sons of God, pre-Christian deities like *gudani* and *lashari*, to whom the mountain people gave special devotion, and it also means "icon" or just "image" (Anderson, 2003, p.97).

The Juhuru, the Mountain Jews of Daghestan, have incorporated many pagan rites and superstitions into their belief system too. For example, in the cycle of wedding, birth, and funeral rituals are a number of pre-Judaic and pre-monotheistic concepts, including belief in the purifying strength of fire, water, amulets, and talismans against evil spirits (water nymphs, devils, etc.).

Num-Negear is the lord of travelers and home life, Ile-Nove is

Ilya the Prophet, Ozhdegoe-Mar is the house spirit, and Ser and Shegadu are malicious spirits. And to honor Gudur-boy and Kesen-boy (the spirits of autumn and spring) the Mountain Jews arranged special festivals. The Shev-Idor celebration is dedicated to Idor, master of the plant kingdom, and for the eve of spring festival girls would practice a form of divination that made use of flowers taken from forests (adapted from http://russia.rin.ru/guides_e/4753.html [accessed 6/8/08]).

The Mountain Jews would also perform what is known as the *gudil* ceremony, which has two functions: to appeal for rain during a drought or, conversely, to bring excessive rains to an end.

> Until recently, children in some regions marched in a noisy procession carrying a *gudil* figure – a scarecrow made of branches and rags. The procession wound its way past all the Jewish homes, where young women laughed and older women recited prayers. All distributed presents to the children and poured cold water on the scarecrow, hoping the rain would similarly quench the land (see Mikdash-Shamailov, 2002, p.117).

Sometimes the child was replaced by an adult member of the community dressed as a scarecrow, and when the appeal was for sunshine, the scarecrow was colored red.

Although they are basically monotheistic, the Mountain Jews also believe in the existence of supernatural forces, but under God's dominion: "These forces may be visible, and some take on the form of animals. They have the power to punish people for their sins and reward them for their good deeds. While some have permanent features, others change in appearance and character according to a person's behaviour" (Mikdash-Shamailov, 2002, p.112).

These supernatural beings include *She'atu* – "an evil spirit that stirs in the dark and often appears in deserted houses, near water sources, in open fields, or in the thick of forests" (Mikdash-Shamailov, 2002, p.112). There is also *Num-ne-gir* (which translates as "she whose name shall not be uttered") who "is associated with fertility and family happiness. She is also responsible for the safety of travellers. Her name remains unspoken because it inspires great fear" (Mikdash-Shamailov, 2002, pp.112-113). Then there is the spirit of the Water Mother, known as *Ser-ovi* or *Dedei-ovi,* who "lures lovers or pregnant women to a river in which they disappear forever" (Mikdash-Shamailov, 2002, p.113).

Belief in the evil eye is widespread among the Juhur too, with people attempting to counter its effect by carrying amulets prepared by rabbis or healers, or verses copied from the Talmud.

> Healers are thought to have the ability to understand and cure physical weaknesses, a condition usually attributed to the evil eye. One method they use is to throw balls of dough into a fire while calling out the names of all enemies known to the patient. If the balls burn without exploding or bouncing out of the fire, the evil eye is not to blame. If a ball explodes when the name of an enemy is called out, the healer must rip off a piece of the enemy's garment, burn it, let the patient inhale the smoke, and sprinkle the patient's forehead with the ash. The evil eye can also be thwarted by reading a glass of water. Wax or melted lead is tossed into the water, and the ensuing form is believed to closely resemble the person who caused the illness. Salt is then scattered over a fire, blinding – or even destroying – the enemy whose image is revealed (Mikdash-Shamailov, 2002, p.111).

Additionally, they also celebrate a Spring Festival, called Shegme-Vasal (the Spring Candle), in which the element of fire plays a special role.

> Young people in Daghestan customarily skip over a campfire and chant songs of supplication, asking to be protected from the evil eye, their fields shielded from drought during the planting season, and their animals spared from the cattle plague. The

> campfire is lit on the site of an abandoned threshing floor to ensure that the coming year will be fertile" (Mikdash-Shamailov, 2002, pp.85-86).

We can find examples of such practices in present day Armenia too. For example, there is a pagan goddess of water, and a festival is still held in her honor each year:

> [E]ach year at Armenia's only remaining pagan temple, at Garni, 32 kilometers east of Yerevan, a few hundred Armenians gather to celebrate Vardavar as an event that they consider represents Armenians' true and original faith. The festival is perhaps the most popular of all traditional and religious events in the Armenian calendar, with youngsters and adults gleefully dumping water over hapless passers-by. The celebration has now been absorbed into the Christian calendar, but was traditionally associated with Astghik, the Armenian goddess of water, beauty, love and fertility. The festival's name is derived from the Armenian word for rose, "vard." Early observers of Vardavar offered Astghik roses and sprinkled water on each other, or feasted near water in the hope that she would provide rain in time for harvest. Now re-invented to represent the transfiguration of Christ, the holiday is scheduled by the Armenian Church to be held approximately 98 days after Easter. (From an article by Onnik Krikorian, a journalist and photographer from the United Kingdom living and working in the Republic of Armenia, first published by Eurasianet, http://www.eurasianet.org, [accessed 13/01/2008]).

So despite the well-documented attempts by the Soviet regime to erase the distinctive features of its member nations and homogenize them into a single Russian model, the peoples of the Caucasus, even those who are still part of the Russian Federation, have managed to maintain many of their traditional customs, and the stories in this collection reflect this.

Some, coming from more orthodox backgrounds, find the eclectic mix of beliefs held by the peoples of the Caucasus hard to come to terms with. The following poem by the great Turkish sufist and philosopher poet Mawlana Jalal'ad Din Rumi puts the issue in perspective:

> What can I do, Submitters to God? I do not know myself.
> I am neither Christian nor Jew, neither Zoroastrian nor Muslim,
> I am not from east or west, not from land or sea,
> not from the shafts of nature nor from the spheres of the firmament,
> not of the earth, not of water, not of air, not of fire.
> I am not from the highest heaven, not from this world,
> not from existence, not from being.
> I am not from India, not from China, not from Bulgar, not from Saqsin,
> not from the realm of the two Iraqs, not from the land of Khurasan
> I am not from the world, not from beyond,
> not from heaven and not from hell.
> I am not from Adam, not from Eve, not from paradise and not from Ridwan.
> My place is placeless, my trace is traceless,
> no body, no soul, I am from the soul of souls.
> I have chased out duality, lived the two worlds as one.
> One I seek, one I know, one I see, one I call.
> He is the first, he is the last, he is the outer, he is the inner.
> Beyond "He" and "He is" I know no other.
> I am drunk from the cup of love, the two worlds have escaped me.
> I have no concern but carouse and rapture.
> If one day in my life I spend a moment without you

from that hour and that time I would repent my life.
If one day I am given a moment in solitude with you
I will trample the two worlds underfoot and dance forever.
O Sun of Tabriz (Shams Tabrizi), I am so tipsy here in this world,
I have no tale to tell but tipsiness and rapture.

Come, come, whoever you are,
Wanderer, idolater, worshiper of fire,
Come even though you have broken your vows a thousand times,
Come, and come yet again.
Ours is not a caravan of despair.

It was posted to me by Eren Alkan, Faculty of Letters, Ege University, Izmir, Turkey in response to a paper I submitted to the Second International Online Conference on Religious Studies organized by the Moscow Society for the Study of Religions, Faculty of Philosophy, Moscow State University. And here is part of Eren Alkan's commentary on the poem: "I think all disciplines meet at the same place: to breathe. We talk, write, participate, involve, want, etc. for only one aim: to breathe. ... Who we are is not the issue. Only to breathe in a true way can change a word".

***

Let us now return to the shamanic stories themselves and what they have in common, while at the same time bearing in mind that the definition is a polytheistic one. This includes the fact that they are all tales of power, how they generally deal with healing in some form, and how they usually only contain a limited number of characters. As for the style in which they are written, it has aptly been called "magic realism" and this is something the shamanic story shares with fairy tales.

As for shamanic stories of the Caucasus, rather than those found in other parts of the world, the formulaic openings and endings have already been commented upon, and so has the significance of the numbers three and seven. We should also mention how the focus is on action rather than on detailed description, how epithets are commonly used ("King's son" instead of "prince," and "king's daughter" instead of "princess"), the frequent use of the horse as the main means of transport, the importance attached to giving hospitality to guests, and the way in which adversaries often take the form of Narts or Devs.

In addition to the openings and endings, another popular formula often repeated in the stories is "Whether they travelled a long or short time, only God knows." Frequently, the following disclaimer appears too: "Whether it happened or not ..." or "there was and there wasn't..." As well as this being a stylistic device, it also serves to show how in an altered state of consciousness, such as on a shamanic journey, clock time and the rules of ordinary reality no longer apply.

As for the story endings, in Armenia many are a variation on "Three apples fell from heaven – one apple for the storyteller, the second for the person listening to the story, and the third for the whole, wide world" (see Marshall, 2007, p.xxviii). As the apple traditionally represents the gift of immortality, this could perhaps be regarded as the blessing bestowed on storytellers in return for the teachings that they impart to us.

We should also comment upon the way in which the hero, often the youngest of three sons, generally goes through a process of initiation during the course of the action in the same way a shaman would, how this entails passing through barriers, communicating with animals, taking them on as helpers, having to go through some form of transformation or dismemberment, and how all this leads to the equilibrium of the community being restored.

The term "initiation" can be used to denote

> a body of rites and oral teachings whose purpose is to produce a decisive alteration in the religious and social status of the person to be initiated. In philosophical terms, initiation is equivalent to a basic change in existential condition; the novice emerges from his ordeal endowed with a totally different being from that which he possessed before his initiation; he has become another (Eliade, 1958, p.x).

In the same way as the person initiated becomes another by the end of each story, if the tale is a powerful one, so does the reader, and this, as well as providing some entertainment along the way, is surely the ultimate goal of the storyteller.

Bilocation (the apparent ability to be in two places at the same time), having animal familiars and/or healing powers, undertaking spiritual journeys to other worlds, shape-shifting, carrying out soul retrievals, and practicing divination, are all elements to be found in the folktales presented in this collection. Moreover, all are elements typically associated with shamanism too, which point to the fact that shamanism must once have been prevalent in the region. As to the form or forms it took, this we are unable to be specific about, and any attempts to pretend otherwise, in the absence of more concrete evidence, would be nothing more than fraudulent, which is why it has not been attempted here.

Instead it is hoped that this collection will have provided you with a taste of the riches that the region holds, and thus have interested you in both visiting and finding out more about it for yourselves while it still retains its unique character. Do so, and you will undoubtedly be captivated by its charms, in the same way as I have.

Notes

1. The main texts connected with the Shinto tradition are the *Kojiki* (Record of Ancient Matters) and the *Nihon Shoki* (Chronicles of Japan). They were both written in Chinese in the early eighth century to help legitimate the position and the prestige of the Imperial Court but neither can be considered to represent a theology as such.
2. Archaeology tunnels into the deep foundations on which the arrogance of civilizations and revolutions rests. When the tunnelers enter foundations which should be rock but are merely sand, the floors of the state apartments high above them begin to tremble" (Ascherson, 2007, p.76). A good example of this is what we now know about the Scythians. "All knowledge about the Scythains, as it accumulates, has undermined the proposition that the peoples of the Black Sea steppe were primitive and barbarous, and the conclusion that nomadism was a backward form of existence" (Ascherson, 2007, p.76).
3. Despite the criticism now leveled against Eliade's work, without him the current interest in shamanism would probably never have materialized. So instead of dismissing Eliade out of hand as someone who merely popularized various ethnographic reports written by others, by casting a critical eye over what he has to say and by being selective, it is felt there is still a lot of value to be found in his writing and thus justification for referring to it.
4. [E]ach year at Armenia's only remaining pagan temple, at Garni, 32 kilometers east of Yerevan, a few hundred Armenians gather to celebrate Vardavar as an event that they consider represents Armenians' true and original faith. The festival is perhaps the most popular of all traditional and religious events in the Armenian calendar, with youngsters and adults gleefully dumping water over hapless passers-by. The celebration has

now been absorbed into the Christian calendar, but was traditionally associated with Astghik, the Armenian goddess of water, beauty, love and fertility. The festival's name is derived from the Armenian word for rose, "vard." Early observers of Vardavar offered Astghik roses and sprinkled water on each other, or feasted near water in the hope that she would provide rain in time for harvest. Now re-invented to represent the transfiguration of Christ, the holiday is scheduled by the Armenian Church to be held approximately 98 days after Easter. (taken from an article by Onnik Krikorian, a journalist and photographer from the United Kingdom living and working in the Republic of Armenia, first published by Eurasianet, http://www.eurasianet.org [accessed 13/01/2008]).

5. One of the neighboring regions, and bordering Chechnya, is Ingushetia, the second smallest republic of the Russian Federation. It was created in June 1992 as a result of the secession of the Ingush from Checheno-Ingushetia, where the Ingush had been very much in the minority. The decision to break away followed the declaration of independence by the Chechens in 1991. The partition left the Ingush without an urban centre, as all the cultural and educational facilities remained in Chechnya's capital Djohar (formerly Grozny) and the former capital of Ingushetia, Nazran, was unsuitable for the purpose. So a new capital, Magas, was inaugurated in 1998 (see Matveena, 1999, pp.91 & 92).
6. Many Azerbaijanis can also be found in other countries. There are nearly one million living in Russia and another 400,000 in the United States. More than eighteen million ethnic Azerbaijanis live in the Azerbaijan provinces of northern Iran. Most of the people speak Azerbaijani, a language that is closely related to Turkish. It was originally written in Arabic, but since Azerbaijan gained independence a Turkish version of the Roman script has been used (see Kaeter, 2004, p.74).
7. According to Lucy Menzies, who translated *Caucasian Folk-tales*

by Adolf Dirr into English, "*Divs* or *Deevs* are supposed to have been the race of giants who inhabited the world before Adam. They also are supposed to have fallen into sin, and to have been therefore banished by the Almighty to the Caucasus. The heights of Elbruz and Ararat are supposed to be the headquarters of these fabulous giants" (in Dirr, 1925 p.x).

8. The word *Daghestan* or *Daghistan* means "country of mountains", derived from the Turkic word dağ meaning "mountain" and Persian suffix -stan meaning "land of". Most of the Republic is in fact mountainous, with the Greater Caucasus Mountains covering the south and the highest point being the Bazardyuzi peak at 4,466 m.

Bibliography

Abdurakhmanov, A. M. 1992. "Totemistic Elements in Rituals and Legends about Animals." Hewitt, George (ed.), *Caucasian Perspectives*, 392-405. Lincom Europa, Munich.

Alakbarli, F. (2006). *Medical Manuscripts of Azerbaijan*. Baku: HAF.

Allen, W.E.D. (1932). *A History of the Georgian People*. London: Kegan Paul, Trench, Trubner & Co. Ltd.

D'Alviella, G. (1894). *The Migration of Symbols*. London: A. Constable and Co. Scanned, proofed and formatted at sacred-texts.com by John Bruno Hare, September 2008. This text is in the public domain in the US because it was published prior to 1923.

Anchabadze, G. (2001). *The Vainakhs (The Chechens and Ingush)*. Tbilisi: Caucasian House.

Anderson, T. (2003). *Bread and Ashes: A Walk Through the Mountains of Georgia*. London: Jonathan Cape.

Ascherson, N. (2007). *Black Sea: The Birthplace of Civilisation and Barbarism*. London: Vintage Books.

Bal, M. (2004). *Narratology: Introduction to the Theory of Narrative*. Canada: University of Toronto Press.

Beard, M. (1993). *Mythos in mythenloser Gesellschaft: Das aradigma Roms*, 62-64. ed. Fritz Graf (Stuttgart and Leipzig: B.G.Teubner).

Benet, S. (1974). *Abkhasians: Long-Living People of the Caucasus*. New York: Holt, Rinehart and Winston, Inc.

Berg, H. (2001). *Dargi Folktales: Oral stories from the Caucasus and an introduction to Dargi grammar*. Universiteit Leiden, The Netherlands: Research School of Asian, African, and Amerindian Studies.

Berman, M. (2006). "The Nature of Shamanism and the Shamanic Journey," unpublished M.Phil. Thesis, University of Wales, Lampeter.

Berman, M. (2007). *The Nature of Shamanism and the Shamanic Story*.

Newcastle: Cambridge Scholars Publishing.

Berman, M. (2008a). *Soul Loss and the Shamanic Story*. Newcastle: Cambridge Scholars Publishing.

Berman, M. (2008b). *Divination and the Shamanic Story*. Newcastle: Cambridge Scholars Publishing.

Bettelheim, B. (1991). *The Uses of Enchantment*. London: Penguin Books.

Bgazhba, Kh.S. (1985). *Abkhazian Tales,* Translated from the Russian, with new introduction by D.G. Hunt. (Russian edition published by Alashara Publishing House, Sukhumi).

Blair, B (1996). "Wisdom of the Ages-Verbal Folklore." In *Azerbaijan International,* Autumn 1996 (4.3).

Blavatsky, H.P. (1980). "The Number Seven." In *Theosophist,* June, 1880.

Bleichsteiner, R. (1936). "Rossweihe und Pferdererennen in Totenkult der kaukasi-schen Völker." In *Wiener Beiträge zur Kulturgeschichte und Linguistik* IV:413-495.

Bogoras, W. *The Chukchee*. New York: Memoirs of the American Museum of Natural History, vol.11, 1909.

Bonnefoy, Y. (comp.) (1993). *American, African and Old European Mythologies*. Chicago and London, The University of Chicago Press.

Booker, C. (2004). *The Seven Basic Plots: Why we tell Stories*. London: Continuum.

Boyajian, Z.C. (1916). *Armenian Legends and Poems*. London: J.M. Dent & Sons Ltd. Scanned at sacred-texts.com, June 2006. Proofed and formatted by John Bruno Hare. This text is in the public domain in the United States because it was published prior to January 1st, 1923. These files may be used for any non-commercial purpose, provided this notice of attribution is left intact in all copies.

Burney, C., & Lang, D.M. (1971). *The People of the Hills: Ancient Ararat and Caucasus*. London: Phoenix Press.

Calinescu, M. (1978). "The Disguises of Miracle: Notes on Mircea

Eliade's Fiction." In Rennie, Bryan (ed.) (2006), *Mircea Eliade: A Critical Reader*. London: Equinox Publishing Ltd.

Castaneda, C. (1974). *Tales of Power*. New York: Simon and Schuster.

Charachidzé, G. (1968). *Le système religieux de la Géorgie païenne.analyse structurale d'une civilization*. Paris: Maspero.

Chenciner, R. (1997). *Daghestan: Tradition & Survival*. Richmond, Surrey: Curzon Press.

Chenciner, R., Ismailov, G. & Magomedkhanov, M. (2006). *Tattooed Mountain Women and Spoon Boxes of Daghestan*. London: Bennett & Bloom.

Choloq'ashvili, R. (2004). *Imagery and Beliefs in Georgian Folk Tales*. Tbilisi: Nekeri.

Colarusso, J. (1997). "Peoples of the Caucasus." In *Encyclopaedia of Cultures and Daily Life*, Pepper Pike, Ohio: Eastword Publications (taken from www.circassianworld.com [accessed 15/7/08]).

Cooper, J.J. (ed.) (1997). *Brewer's Book of Myth & Legend*. Oxford: Helicon Publishing Ltd.

Cowan, J. (1992.) *Mysteries of the Dream-time: The Spiritual Life of Australian Aborigines*. Bridport, Dorset: Prism Press.

Curtis, W.E. (1911). *Around the Black Sea*. London: Hodder & Stoughton.

Czaplicka, M.A. (2007). *Shamanism in Siberia*. [Excerpts from] *Aboriginal Siberia A Study in Social Anthropology*, Charleston SC: BiblioBazaar (Original Copyright 1914, Oxford).

Dan, J. (2006). *Kabbalah: A very short Introduction*. New York: Oxford University Press.

Diachenko, V. (1994). "The Horse in Yakut Shamanism." In Seaman, G. & Day, J.S., *Ancient Traditions: Shamanism in Central Asia and the Americas*. Boulder, Colorado: University Press of Colorado.

Diakonova, V.P. (1994). "Shamans in Traditional Tuvinian Society." In Seaman, G. & Day, J.S., *Ancient Traditions: Shamanism in Central Asia and the Americas*. Boulder, Colorado: University Press of Colorado.

Dirr, A. (1925). *Caucasian Folk-tales*. Translated into English by Lucy

Menzies, London & Toronto: J.M. Dent & Sons Ltd.

Dolidze, N.I. (1999). *Georgian Folk Tales*. Tbilisi: Merani Publishing House.

Dow, J. (1986). "Universal aspects of symbolic healing: A theoretical synthesis." *American Anthropologist*, 88: 56-69.

Downing, C. (1972.) *Armenian Folk-Tales and Fables*. Oxford: Oxford University Press.

Dragadze, T. (ed.) (2000). *Azerbaijan*. London: Melisende

Driver, T.F. (1991). *The Magic of Ritual*. New York: Harper Collins Publishers.

Dumont, L. (1983). *Essai sur l'individualisme: Une perspective anthropologique sur l'ideologie moderne*. Paris: Editions du Seuil.

Durkheim, É. (2001). *The Elementary Forms of Religious Life*. Oxford: Oxford University Press (originally published in 1912).

Eigner, D. (2008). "Spirit Possession in Central Nepal." In *Shaman* Vol. 16 Nos 1 & 2 Spring/Autumn 2008. Budapest: Molnar and Kelemen Oriental Publishers.

Eliade, M. (1964). *Myth and Reality*. London: George Allen & Unwin

Eliade, M. (1981). *Tales of the Sacred and the Supernatural*. Philadelphia: The Westminster Press.

Eliade, M. (1989). *Shamanism: Archaic techniques of ecstasy*. London: Arkana (first published in the USA by Pantheon Books 1964).

Eliade, M. (1991). *Images and Symbols*. New Jersey: Princeton University Press (The original edition is copyright Librarie Gallimard 1952).

Eliade, M. (2003). *Rites and Symbols of Initiation*. Putnam, Connecticut: Spring Publications (originally published by Harper Bros., New York, 1958).

Frazer, J. (1993). *The Golden Bough*. Ware, Hertfordshire: Wordsworth Editions Ltd (first published in 1922).

Gall, C., & de Waal, T. (1997) *Chechnya: A Small victorious War*, London: Pan Books.

Garnett, L.M.J. (1904). *Turkish Life in Town and Country*. London: G.P. Putnam's Sons.

Gray, J. (2004). "SRM-Atheism – Fanatical Unbelief." *Prospect Magazine* – November 2004.
http://home.infostations.net/srm/athart8.htm
[accessed 25th December 2004].

Griffin, N. (2001). *Caucasus: A Journey to the Land between Christianity and Islam*. Chicago: The University of Chicago Press.

Grof, S. (1994). *Books of the Dead: Manuals for Living and Dying*. London: Thames & Hudson.

Halifax, J. (1991). *Shamanic Voices*. London: Arkana (first published in 1979).

Hallam, M. "The Matrix," in *New View*, Summer 2002. London: The Anthroposophical Association Ltd.

Hansen, G. P. (2001). *The Trickster and the Paranormal*. New York: Xlibris.

Harner, M. (1990). *The Way of the Shaman*, (3rd Edition). Harper & Row (first published by Harper & Row in 1980).

Helman, C. (2006). *Suburban Shaman tales from medicine's frontline*. London: Hammersmith Press.

Hewitt, G. (ed.) (1999). *The Abkhasians: A Handbook*. Richmond, Surrey: Curzon Press.

Hoogasian-Villa, S. (1966). *100 Armenian Tales*. Detroit, Michigan: Wayne State University Press.

Hoskins, J. (1996). "From Diagnosis to Performance: Medical Practice and the Politics of Exchange in Kodi, West Sumba." In Laderman, Carol & Roseman, Marina (eds.), *The Performance of Healing*, 271-290. London: Routledge.

Hultkrantz, A. (1993). "The Shamans in Myths and Tales." In *Shaman* Vol. 1 No. 2. 39-55.

Hunt, D.G. (trans.) (2004). *Folklore of the North West Caucasus and Chechnya*. Tbilisi: Caucasus House.

Hunt, D.G. (trans.) (2005). *The Heroic Epos of the Chechens and Ingush*. (Unpublished and in loose leaf format in the British Library. Russian edition published by Nauka, 1972 for the A.M. Gorky Institute of World Literature).

Hunt, D.G. (2006) "Colour Symbolism in the Folk Literature of the Caucasus." In *Folklore*, Vol. 117, 2006.

Hunt, D.G. (2007). *Avar folk tales*. Compiled, translated from Avar and with commentary by D.M. Ataev; translated from the Russian with new introduction by D.G. Hunt. Russian edition published by Nauka, Moscow, 1971 as part of their series: "Tales and myths of Oriental peoples" (in loose leaf format in the British Library).

Ibragimov, M. (ed.) (1977). *Azerbaijanian Prose*. Moscow: Progress Publishers.

Jaimoukha, A.M. (2005). *The Chechens: A Handbook*. New York; London: Routledge Curzon.

Jung, C.G. (1977). *The Symbolic Life*. London and Henley: Routledge & Keegan Paul.

Kaeter, M. (2004). *The Caucasian Republics*. New York: Facts On File, Inc.

King, C. (2008). *The Ghost of Freedom*. New York: Oxford University Press Inc.

Kremer, J.W. (1988). "Shamanic Tales as Ways of Personal Empowerment." In Doore, Gary (ed.), *Shaman's Path: Healing, Personal Growth and Empowerment,* 189-199. Boston, Massachusetts: Shambhala Publications.

Lévi-Strauss, C. (1968). *Structural Anthropology*. Harmondsworth: Penguin.

Lewis, I.M. (2003). *Ecstatic Religion: a study of shamanism and spirit possession,*

3rd Edition. London: Routledge (first published 1971 by Penguin Books).

Lyle, E. (2007). "Narrative Form and the Structure of Myth." in *Folklore* 33, 59.

Maddox, J. L. (2003). *Shamans and Shamanism*. Dover Publications Inc. (originally published in 1923 by the Macmillan Company, New York, under the title *The Medicine Man: A Sociological Study of the Character and Evolution of Shamanism*).

Malsagov, A.O. (2007). *Tales of the Ingush and Chechens.* (Russian edition published by Nauka, Moscow, 1983 as part of their series: "Tales and myths of Oriental peoples").

Marchand, L. (ed.) (1976). *Byron, Letters and Journals,* vol. V. London: Harvard University Press.

Marshall, Bonnie C. (2007). *The Flower of Paradise And Other Armenian Tales.* Westport, CT: Libraries Unlimited.

Mathews, F. (1994). *The Ecological Self.* London: Routledge.

Matveena, A. (1999). *The North Caucasus: Russia's Fragile Borderland.* London: The Royal Institute of International Affairs.

Mikdash-Shamailov, L. (ed.) (2002). *Mountain Jews: Customs and Daily Life in the Caucasus.* Jerusalem: The Israel Museum.

Naysmith, P. (1998). *The Wardrops: A legacy of Britain in Georgia.* The British Council (the catalogue that accompanied a British Council Exhibition that toured Georgia in 1998).

Nioradze, G. (1940). "Micvalebulis haerze damarxva." ENIMKI-s moambe V-VI: 57-81.

Ochiauri, T. (1954). "Kartvelta udzvelesi sarc'munoebis ist'oriidan." (From the history of the ancient religion of the Georgians) Tbilisi: Mecniereba.

Papashvily, G., & Papashvily, H. (1946). *Yes and No Stories: A Book of Georgian Folk Tales.* New York: Harper & Brothers.

Pattee, R. (1988). "Ecstasy and Sacrifice." In Doore, Gary (ed.), *Shaman's Path: Healing, Personal Growth and Empowerment,* 17–31. Boston, Massachusetts: Shambhala Publications.

Pearce, B. (1954). "The Ossetians In History." In Rothstein, A. (Ed.) (1954), *A People Reborn: The Story of North Ossetia,* 12-17. London: Lawrence & Wishart.

Rennie, B. S. (1996). *Reconstructing Eliade: making sense of religion.* Albany: State University of New York Press.

Ripinsky-Naxon, M. (1993). *The Nature of Shamanism.* Albany: State University of New York Press.

Ruck, Carl A.P., Staples, B.D., Celdran J.A.G., Hoffman, M.A. (2007). *The Hidden World: Survival of Pagan Shamanic Themes in European*

Fairytales. North Carolina: Carolina Academic Press.

Rutherford, W. (1986). *Shamanism: The Foundations of Magic*. Wellingborough, Northamptonshire: The Aquarian Press.

Segal, R.A. (2004). *Myth: A Very Short Introduction*. Oxford: Oxford University Press.

Seligman, M.E.P. (1975). *Helplessness: On Depression, development, and death*. San Francisco: Freeman.

Sikala, A.L. (1992). "Understanding narratives of the 'other'." In Kvideland, R. (ed.), *Folklore Processed*. Helsinki: Suomalaisen Kirjallisuuden Seura.

Smith, J.Z. (1982). *Imagining Religion: From Babylon to Jonestown*. Chicago: University of Chicago Press.

Smith, S. (2006). *Allah's Mountains: The Battle for Chechnya*. London: Tauris Parke Paperbacks.

Surmelian L. Z. (1968). *Apples of immortality: folktales of Armenia*. London: George Allen and Unwin Ltd.

Taube, E. (1984) "South Siberian and Central Asian Hero Tales and Shamanistic Rituals." In Hoppál, Mihály (ed.), *Shamanism in Eurasia*, Part 1, 344-352. Göttingen, Edition Herodot.

Tuite, K. (ed.) (1995). *Violet on the Mountain: An Anthology of Georgian Folk Poetry*. Tbilisi: Amirani.

Tuite, K. (2004). "Highland Georgian paganism—archaism or innovation?" Review of Zurab K'ik'nadze 1996, *Kartuli Mitologia, I. Δvari da saq'mo*. (Georgian Mythology, I. The cross and his people [*sic*], Kutaisi: Gelati Academy of Sciences; for the Annual of the Society for the Study of the Caucasus. http://www. mapageweb.umontreal.ca/ tuitekj/publications/ Shamanism Acetates.pdf. [accessed 29/10/07].

Tuite, K (2006). "The Meaning of Dael Symbolic and Spatial Associations of the South Caucasian Goddess of Game Animals." In O'Neil, C., Scoggin, M. & Tuite, K. (eds.), *Language, Culture and the Individual*. Muenchen: Lincom Europa.

Turner, H.W. (1971). *Living Tribal Religions*. London: Ward Lock Educational.

Turner, V. (1981). *Drums of Affliction*. London: Hutchinson University Library for Africa (first published in 1968).

Turner, V. (1982). *From Ritual to Theatre: The Human Seriousness of Play*. New York: PAJ Publications (a division of Performing Arts Journal, Inc.).

Turner, V. (1985). *On the Edge of the Bush: Anthropology as Experience.* Tucson, AZ: University of Arizona Press.

Turner, V. (1995). *The Ritual Process: Structure and Anti-Structure.* Chicago, Illinois: Aldine Publishing Company (first published in 1969).

Ussher, J. (1865). *A Journey from London to Persepolis*. London: Hurst & Blackett.

Vaday, A. (2002). "The World of Beliefs of the Sarmatians." A Nógrád Megyei Múzeumok Évkönyve XXVI.

Van Gennep, A. (1977). *The Rites of Passage*. London: Routledge and Keegan Paul (original work published in 1909).

Vinogradov, A. (2002). "The Role and Development of Shamanistic Discourse among Southern Siberian Ethnic groups in the post-Soviet period." In *The Anthropology of East Europe Review*, vol.20 No.2.

Vitebsky, P. (2001). *The Shaman*. London: Duncan Baird (first published in Great Britain in 1995 by Macmillan Reference Books).

Walker, C.J. (1997). *Visions of Ararat: Writings on Armenia*. London: I.B.Tauris.

Wallis, R.J. (2003). *Shamans/Neo-shamans*. London: Routledge.

Walsh, R.N. (2007). *The World of Shamanism: New Views of an Ancient Tradition*. Woodbury, Minnesota: Llewellyn Publicaions.

Wardrop, M. (1894). *Georgian Folk Tales*. London: David Nutt.

Winkelman, M. (2000). *Shamanism: The Neural Ecology of Consciousness and Healing*. Westport, Connecticut: Bergin & Garvey.

Winterbourne, A. (2007). *When The Norns Have Spoken: Time and Fate in Germanic Paganism*. Wales: Superscript.

Znamenski, A.A. (2007). *The Beauty of the Primitive: Shamanism and the Western Imagination*. Oxford: University Press.

Index